A HOUSE

TO REMEMBER

10

RILLINGTON PLACE

Edna E Gammon

A
HOUSE
TO REMEMBER

10
RILLINGTON PLACE

DEDICATED TO THE MEMORY OF
BERYL AND GERALDINE EVANS

Edited by Chris Newton

MEMOIRS
Cirencester

Published by Memoirs

MEMOIRS

Memoirs Books

25 Market Place, Cirencester, Gloucestershire, GL7 2NX
info@memoirsbooks.co.uk www.memoirsbooks.co.uk

ISBN 978-1-908223-38-8

Printed and bound in Great Britain by
Marston Book Services Ltd, Oxfordshire

A HOUSE TO REMEMBER

10
RILLINGTON PLACE

Contents

Introduction

In January 1950, Timothy Evans was found guilty of the murder of his baby daughter at the family home, a top-floor flat at 10 Rillington Place, Notting Hill. He was also assumed to have killed his wife Beryl. Evans was hanged in March of that year.

Only long after Evans had been executed was it discovered that another tenant, John Christie, a key witness at Evans' trial, had already murdered at least two other women in the house; their bodies had been buried in the garden. After Evans' execution Christie had resumed the killing and gone on to murder four more women, including his own wife Ethel. These women would probably have been saved if the police investigation into the Evans case had not been badly bungled and the bodies of Christie's earlier victims overlooked.

Christie was eventually arrested and charged in March 1953, after a subsequent tenant found the bodies of his last three victims behind a dummy wall in the kitchen. Christie was hanged for his crimes later that year.

In 1966, on the basis that Evans' conviction was unsafe and it appeared more likely that Christie had killed Geraldine Evans, if not Beryl, Timothy Evans was granted a posthumous pardon.

Many people have continued to believe that Evans was innocent and that Christie must have been responsible for the murders of Beryl and Geraldine Evans (he claimed to have murdered Beryl, though his account of the killing was contradicted by the post-mortem evidence) as well as the other women who died at 10 Rillington Place.

Having studied the case in great detail, I do not believe this. I think 10 Rillington Place housed two murderers, and that Timothy Evans' original guilty sentence was correct.

It was said that having two murderers living in the same house was impossible. I do not believe that. Murder has no boundaries.

This is the story of two men - one a perverted monster who was able to live with his victims and found satisfaction in their dead bodies, the other a young man whose marriage was failing. Finding it difficult to cope with all the pressures surrounding him, he suddenly lost control. I believe that while the balance of his mind was disturbed, Evans did indeed commit murder.

This book is the author's own version of what may have taken place at 10 Rillington Place between 1943 and 1953.

Chapter One

A MEETING OF MURDERERS

Beryl Susanna Thorley was born on September 19 1929 at 390, High Street, Lewisham, London. This institution was part charitable hospital, part workhouse. Most of it was destroyed during World War II by a V1 bomb. A new hospital now stands near the site.

Beryl's father was William Thorley, a petrol pump attendant. As far as is known he died in November 1963, when he was living in Brighton.

Her mother was Elizabeth Simmonds, a housekeeper in Lewisham. Very little is known about her. During Beryl's life, and especially after she was married, her mother was always referred to as having died.

Nothing is known about Beryl's childhood and early teens, so we have to fast forward to when she was about 17 years old and living in Cambridge Gardens, Kensington, London. She had grown into a lovely girl and was working as a telephonist in Grosvenor House, Mayfair. To be employed at this hotel, one had to come up to a very high standard. You needed a good education and a smart appearance.

Timothy John Evans was born in Merthyr Vale on November 20 1924. Daniel Evans, his father, was a coal haulier. Thomasina, his mother, was pregnant with Evans when his father walked out on the family and was never seen or heard of again. Timothy had an older sister, Eileen.

In 1929 Mrs Evans got married again, to a Penry Probert, and they had a daughter, Maureen.

Timothy Evans had a violent temper, and would fly off the handle if he did not get his own way. It soon became evident that he was also a habitual liar; his family never knew when he was telling the truth and when he was lying. He certainly did not like going to school, and his headmaster complained many times about him playing truant.

One day while bathing in a river he cut his foot, which became infected, requiring frequent hospital treatment. This resulted in him having to miss quite a lot of his schooling.

During the 1930s the family moved to London, because Mr Probert had found a better job. Evans did not like this at all, so he was sent back to Merthyr Vale to live with his grandmother. How much control she had of this young boy is not known; probably very little. It was always claimed by his family that he was unable to read or write because of his missed schooling, but I would doubt this, as will be discussed later.

When Evans was older he went back to live with his mother at 11 St Marks Road, Notting Hill, London, and found a job as a lorry driver. He liked drinking, going to the cinema and betting on the dogs. He spent a great deal of his spare time at his local pub, the Kensington Park Hotel, where he would indulge in his lies and tell them to all who were prepared to listen.

One of these lies was that his brother (he did not have a brother) was a wealthy Italian count with a fleet of cars, and Evans himself boasted he could have any woman he wanted.

How well this brash young man hit it off with his stepfather is not known - one can only guess. He was always short of money and was not above borrowing it, but never paid it back.

Timothy Evans met Beryl Thorley on a blind date, and was immediately attracted to her. He took her home to meet his mother and two sisters, Eileen and Maureen, who found Beryl to be naïve and immature. Nevertheless, after a short courtship, the couple were married on the September 20 1947 at Kensington Register Office. She had just turned 18 years old. Evans' mother paid all the wedding expenses.

The couple went to live at Mrs Probert's house in St Marks Road, where they were given a back bedroom. Living in the same house were his stepfather, his mother and his two sisters. There was also tenants on the top floor, which his mother had rented out. One can only imagine that there was some tension, all the more so when Beryl quickly became pregnant. It was obvious that they now had to find a place of their own, and it was his elder sister Eileen who told them of a flat to let at 10 Rillington Place.

Without delay, Evans and his wife made their way to Rillington Place, Notting Hill, a cul-de-sac with a row of shabby houses on each side. No 10 was the last house on the left, flanked by a high wall, on the other side of which was an old foundry. It was a grimy, dirty-looking house, one of the shabbiest in the road, and the years of neglect were obvious, but this young couple did not have any choice.

When the front door opened in response to their knock, they met the man who would indirectly destroy both their lives: John Reginald Halliday Christie.

John Christie was born on the April 8 1898 just outside Halifax. His father, Ernest John Christie, was a carpet designer, and he ruled the household with a rod of iron. Christie's mother was apparently a truly lovely lady. She had seven children in all, Percy, Florence, Winnie, Effie and Dolly; a fifth daughter died in infancy. Christie had a high IQ and was a model student at school; he was particularly good at maths. His teachers always praised his work. Christie sang in the church choir and joined the Scouts. Christie grew up dominated by his sisters, but his father was a tyrant and Christie was terrified of him.

When their grandfather died, the children were taken against their mother's wishes to see the body laid out in the coffin. The effect this had on the young Christie, who was only eight at the time, would become clear as the years went by. While his friends played in the parks, John would go off on his own to explore the surrounding cemeteries. He would draw dead bodies and coffins.

At the age of fifteen he got a job as a cinema operator and seemed to be happy with the work. Many other boys of his age were experiencing sexual encounters with the local girls, but Christie was reluctant. However on one occasion a girl took him down a lonely lane and tried to have sex with him, but Christie found it impossible to perform. She went on to spread it around and they taunted him with names like 'Reggie-No-Dick' and 'Can't-Make-It-Christie'. This increased his hatred of the opposite sex.

As Christie grew older he sought the company of prostitutes, whom he of course paid for their services. There was no danger of them taunting him over his performance.

During the 1914-1918 War, Christie served in the Army. While he was on service in France, a mustard gas explosion knocked him unconscious. Following this he always claimed that he had been blinded for several months and had lost his voice. However, there was never any evidence to support this, at least not to the extent Christie claimed.

At the end of his Army service in 1919 he was given a small disability pension and thereafter suffered from an imaginary medical condition, clearly showing signs of a disturbed personality. On his return to Halifax he again took a job as a cinema operator.

In 1920 he became friendly with Ethel Simpson Waddington, a down-to-earth lady who was not concerned over Christie's sexual failures. She herself was no oil painting, and she offered him a life safe from all the trashy females who had taunted him. They married on May 10 1920, and for a short time Christie was content. He got a job as a postman and began stealing postal orders and other items. When his crimes were eventually discovered he was sentenced to three months in prison.

In 1923 Christie was bound over for obtaining money on false pretences and put on probation for twelve months. After this he started consorting once more with prostitutes. Ethel tried to stop their marriage from falling apart by taking her husband to live in Sheffield with her relatives, but this was not at all what he wanted. He left Sheffield and Ethel and returned to London.

Christie spent some time in hospital after being knocked down by a car. This slowed him down for several months, and from then on he was constantly in trouble with the law. There were charges of larceny which led to another six months in prison. In 1929 he had left Ethel and was living with a prostitute. During one of their frequent rows he struck this woman with her son's cricket bat, resulting in her needing several stitches to her head. He protested it was an accident, but for this he went to prison and hard labour for six months.

On his release Christie continued his life of crime, stealing a car from a priest who had befriended him and winding up in prison again. Ethel paid him a visit while he was there and he begged her to return to him on his release. She agreed - a fateful decision on her part.

They found lodgings in Notting Hill and Christie got himself a job as a ledger clerk. In 1938 the Christies moved into the ground floor flat at 10 Rillington Place, a shabby Victorian house which was long past the age when it should have been demolished. There was no bathroom, and only an outside lavatory which was shared by all the tenants. There was a wash-house with a broken-down copper boiler and a filthy sink with a cold water tap, used to rinse out the buckets after emptying their waste down the lavatory. The Christies were given sole use of the garden, which was like a rubbish tip.

On the first floor a Mr Kitchener, a retired railwayman, lived; he had been in this house since 1920. The top floor at this time was unoccupied.

In 1939, at the start of World War II, Christie enrolled as a special constable. It is obvious that a check was not made on his past criminal record, maybe because there was a shortage of men at the home front. Christie, it was said, made a fine job of his duties, and during the blitz of 1940 he helped rescue people who had been bombed out and injured during London's air raids. He had to deal with dead bodies, which presumably excited him.

In 1943 Christie began an affair with a woman who worked at the same police station. When her husband, who was in the Army, came home on leave and was told of the gossip regarding Christie and his wife, he set out to catch them both. When he caught Christie he gave him a severe beating, something Christie did not forget in a hurry. He was later cited in the man's divorce case.

In August 1943 he met a 17-year-old girl called Ruth Fuerst, an Austrian student nurse who also worked as a prostitute. Ethel at the time was away on one of her frequent holidays with her relatives in Sheffield. Ruth Fuerst went to 10 Rillington Place with Christie and was willing to have sex with him. While they were having sex he impulsively strangled her.

His plan to bury her in the garden was interrupted by a telegram from Ethel saying she was on her way home with her brother Henry, who would be staying with them overnight. Henry slept in the front room, where Christie had put Fuerst's body under the floor boards. During the following week, under cover of darkness, he managed to bury her in the garden.

At the end of 1943 Christie left the police force and went to work at the Ultra Radio Works, where he met his second victim, 32-year-old Muriel Eady. Muriel, who lived with her aunt in Putney, was not a prostitute. She suffered badly from catarrh. Christie invited her and her boyfriend to tea. Muriel met Ethel and for a short time the four struck up a friendly relationship.

Christie had to bide his time over Eady, which irritated him; again he had to wait for Ethel to go off on another visit to Sheffield. Finally she left and Christie lost no time in getting to work. He enticed Eady to his flat, saying he could help with her catarrh. He had constructed a device which consisted of a glass jar with a metal top containing two holes. Into one of these he fed a rubber tube which was connected to a gas point in the wall, a bulldog clip obstructing the flow of gas until Christie was ready to release it. The glass jar contained a mixture of Friars Balsam.

Christie put a cardboard mask on Muriel's face, into which he fed the second tube. While Muriel inhaled this mixture Christie released the bulldog clip from the gas tube and she soon lost consciousness. Christie then carried her to the bedroom, removed her knickers and had intercourse with her, strangling her in the process.

His murderous, perverted feelings had again been satisfied. When darkness fell he buried Muriel Eady alongside Ruth Fuerst in the garden.

Christie then went on to seek out further prostitutes. He strongly objected to paying for his pleasure, but at least there was no taunting.

Marriage to Ethel was far from what Christie wanted, and during the later years of their marriage he became more and more irritated with her. However, she was always there to back him up when the need arose and he was able to manipulate her to his own needs. Ethel gave him a life of respectability, and as long as she carried on with her frequent visits to Sheffield he could pursue the darker side of his life.

Chapter Two

THE HOUSE OF DEATH

It was Easter 1948 and a spring sun was shining as Beryl and Timothy Evans stood outside 10 Rillington Place waiting for a response to their knock on the door. Beryl was pregnant, and the couple had been anxiously looking for somewhere to live.

The man who opened the door was John Reginald Halliday Christie. Evans politely asked if they could view the vacant flat, and they were invited into a small, gloomy hallway.

Ethel appeared and they were introduced. She noticed that Beryl was pregnant and pointed out that the flat was on the top floor - could she manage the two flights of stairs? Beryl said she could.

As they went up the narrow uncarpeted stairs, Christie told them about Mr Kitchener, the elderly man who lived on the first floor. He was waiting to go into hospital for an operation on his eyes, and he was very quiet and kept to himself. Later on Mr Kitchener would claim that both Christie and Evans stole from him.

On reaching the top floor Christie showed them two small, dirty rooms. There was a fireplace with an old-fashioned range built into it, a sink with one cold-water tap and a gas stove which was long past its sell-by date. He went on to say that the only lavatory was in the backyard and next to it was the wash-house with a sink and a cold water tap, which was used to rinse out slop pails. There was no access to the garden, as he and his wife had sole use of it. He would collect the rent every Friday on behalf of the agents.

As they did not have any furniture, Evans bought £100 worth on hire purchase. His mother, Mrs Probert, stood as guarantor for them. His sister

Eileen helped Beryl to clean up the flat as best they could and wash down the walls.

Evans was a lorry driver for Lancaster Foods, so his claim that he was illiterate could not be entirely true. He must have been able to make out details of his deliveries and read road signs to hold down this kind of work.

Their marriage, as far as is known, seemed to be happy up to the time when baby Geraldine was born in October 1948. Evans worked long hours, so he did not see much of his baby daughter. Beryl and Timothy went to the cinema every Wednesday night, while Mrs Probert took care of Geraldine, whom she adored as she was her only grandchild.

The cinema would appear to be the only pleasure Beryl had. But Evans went out almost every night to his local pub, the Kensington Park Hotel, and he went regularly to the dog track. He also smoked a lot. His family claimed that Beryl was a poor housekeeper, did not clean the flat and rarely made a hot meal for Evans, also that she did not keep baby Geraldine clean.

For them to believe all this Evans must have set out to belittle Beryl to his family. Why did he do this? It is hardly a sign of a happy marriage. Knowing as we do that Evans was a compulsive liar, we may doubt how much of it was true.

By this stage in their marriage Evans was not above lashing out at Beryl. The Christies and close neighbours heard the frequent rows, and some said he had hit her in the street.

Beryl had great difficulty in making ends meet, especially after the arrival of the baby, and one has to wonder why it was necessary for her to collect £5 of Evans' wages each week from his employer. To help out with the finances Beryl took a part-time job in a shop. Ethel Christie looked after Geraldine, but this arrangement was short lived. One day she told Evans that a work colleague had quite innocently kissed her. He accused her of having an affair and went to her place of work, where he created a violent scene. He was threatened with the police if he did not leave. The result of this was that Beryl lost her job and her much-needed income.

By this time the Christies had heard so many rows and Beryl had complained so often that Evans was hitting her that they must have wondered where all this was going to end. Beryl made no secret of the fact that she wanted to leave Evans, but the Christies could only advise her to seek help. They felt it was not for them to interfere.

Beryl was not helped by the conditions she was living under. By today's standards, what she had to cope with must have been a nightmare for such a young girl. Every drop of hot water had to be boiled in a kettle or pan for the washing of baby Geraldine's nappies, plus their own clothes, and there was no access to the garden for drying. Several times a day she had to go up and down two flights of stairs to empty the waste down the outside toilet. On top of all this, rationing was still in force, so she had the task of making the food last from week to week, as you were only allowed so much on each ration book.

When Lucy Endecott, one of Beryl's school friends, came to stay with her for a few days, Evans had to sleep on the kitchen floor. He complained to his mother over this several times and she said she would put an end to this situation. Beryl for some reason suspected Evans was making advances towards Lucy, and she confronted them both over this. A furious row broke out, with Evans pushing Beryl towards an open window in the kitchen and threatening to throw her out. Both the close neighbours, Mrs Hyde and Mrs Rosina Swan, witnessed this, and also heard the shouting. To make matters worst Evans' mother suddenly appeared on the scene and a fight broke out between her and Lucy Endecott.

The result was that Evans' mother told Lucy she had to leave immediately. Evans responded that if she went, he was going too. Evans packed a suitcase and left with Lucy, followed in hot pursuit by his mother.

The Christies had heard all this row and were standing in the hallway when all three came galloping down the stairs. Finally a tearful Beryl came down, saying she was going to call the police. Ethel saw the state she was in and told Christie to go with her to the nearest phone box.

When the police arrived, Beryl told them she wanted a separation from Evans. All they could do was advise her to see a probation officer, which she apparently did the next day. What took place between the probation officer and Beryl is unknown, and was not made public.

Two days later Evans returned to 10 Rillington Place. He had been sleeping with Lucy Endecott. It was said that Lucy had ordered him out of her lodgings; she later said she had had more of him than she could stand. He had made threats to her, saying he would run her down in his works van. Beryl had no choice but to take Evans back, as he was her only means of support and she had baby Geraldine to consider.

In August 1949 Beryl missed a period, but she put it down to all the stress she had been going through. Then she missed a further two and realised to her horror she was three months pregnant. Geraldine was barely ten months old, and the thought of having another baby with Evans was unimaginable.

When she told Evans about the pregnancy, he commented that she had one child so another wouldn't make any difference. What sort of a man was this? He was heavily in debt, owing money left, right and centre, and it was well known in the neighbourhood that he never paid it back.

Beryl made it clear she was not going through with this pregnancy. She tried using a syringe, which was very painful, and took various tablets at the same time, but to no avail.

Beryl had heard rumours that at one time the Christies had carried out illegal abortions. The police made a thorough investigation, but they found no evidence to support these allegations and the Christies were not charged. Beryl next made enquiries about a woman nearby who would do it for £1.

Beryl confided in Ethel over her unwanted pregnancy, in the hope that she might be able to help her. Ethel also noticed how ill Beryl was beginning to look, thanks to her actions in using a syringe and taking tablets. As a woman she knew that now that Beryl was in her fourth month of pregnancy there was little that could be done, as it would prove to be dangerous. Of course in those days the only option a woman had was a back-street abortion. Ethel of course told Christie of her conversation with Beryl.

Evans claimed that when he arrived home one evening he had been approached by Christie, who had said that he could have aborted Beryl without any risk if they had come to him sooner. The methods that were used carried a 1 in 10 risk of death. He claimed Christie went on to show him medical books. Evans said he could not read and was not interested in any of this and left Christie.

I do not believe this. Beryl was in her fourth month. Christie knew this and would have none of it. I believe Evans only saw a medical book earlier, when Beryl was pregnant with Geraldine. She was on her own all day, but the Christies assured Evans that all would be well if Beryl went into labour while he was away from home. Christie himself was qualified in first aid and Beryl would be all right until the ambulance arrived. I believe it was only then that Evans was shown a St John's Ambulance medical book.

Christie had a framed first-aid certificate on the wall in his front room, and he showed this to Evans to put his mind at ease over Beryl.

In one of Evans' statements he said that on Monday November 7 1949 Beryl had told him when he arrived home from work that she had talked to Christie during the day and he had agreed to abort her baby. Evans said he wanted nothing to do with it, but Beryl told him to mind his own business, and to avoid a further row he went to bed.

On Tuesday November 8 1949 Evans said that he went off to work as usual and Beryl told him on his way out to tell Christie that 'everything had been arranged' for today.

Around this time workmen had started repairing the wash-house roof, and a carpenter was about to take up some rotten floorboards in the hallway and in Christie's front room. At lunchtime on November 8 a woman called Joan Vincent, who was friendly with Beryl, called to see her, but when she knocked on the kitchen door she got no reply. Later she would claim that she had had a feeling that there was someone behind the door. This was not true, as Beryl had gone out earlier with the baby in her pram, accompanied by an unknown woman. Mr Jones, one of the workmen, confirmed he saw them leave. Furthermore Beryl had told the Christies that she had no wish to see Joan as she was a troublemaker.

None of the workmen saw Beryl return home, so it must have been well after 5.30 pm when she got back. Christie had gone to his doctor and Ethel went to the library. Evans had not yet come home from work. Beryl, as always, left the baby's pram in the hallway and went upstairs.

When Evans arrived home at about 7 pm the Christies were already home and met him in the hallway, saying that Beryl was looking very ill and he should see to it that she saw her doctor. The reply they got from Evans was that he would try. He then disappeared upstairs. Ethel was not happy with Evans' response.

Within a short time I believe a furious row broke out, with Beryl lashing out at her husband. Having just finished work, he was in no mood for this. The shouting must have upset baby Geraldine, making her cry. Then Evans struck Beryl in the face with the back of his hand, causing her to stagger backwards. This is my own version of what may have taken place that night, taking into account all the relevant facts. It also takes into account Evans' second statement at Notting Hill Police Station.

Beryl must have come back at him fighting for all she was worth. Evans then lost control; all the anger and frustration suddenly flared up. Unable to stop himself, he delivered a blow with his fist straight into Beryl's face, knocking her to the floor. Evans' fury must have been horrific.

He then got a sash cord from the cupboard drawer and strangled Beryl as she lay helpless on the floor. She must have put up a bitter death struggle, judging by the bruises on her thighs at the post-mortem.

Geraldine's crying by now must have been getting louder. Evans took off his tie and strangled his baby daughter, perhaps from sheer anger – or perhaps because he realised that if he was going to try to conceal the fact that Beryl was dead it would be impossible to account for the baby being there on its own.

One can only guess that Evans sat there for some time before he realised what he had done. We will never know if he made any attempts to revive his wife and daughter.

The Christies must have heard the fighting, as well as baby Geraldine's crying, but they chose to leave well alone. During the night they were awoken by a loud thud which they said later seemed to have come from Evans' flat, plus the sound of something being dragged across the floor. Christie said he went out into the backyard to look up at Evans' window. The light was still on, but there was no sound.

Chapter Three

COVER-UP

The next day, Wednesday November 9 1949, Evans went to work as usual. It seems that the noise the Christies said they had heard during the night must have been Evans wrapping up Beryl's body in the green kitchen tablecloth. The story he later told of Christie helping him to put her body in Mr Kitchener's flat is implausible. The old man was due back from hospital at any time and to find dead bodies in his flat would have given him rather a shock.

I believe Evans kept the bodies of his wife and daughter in his own flat until he could find a way to dispose of them. During that Wednesday Evans came home twice, once at lunchtime and then again later on in the afternoon, to ask Mr Jones when the workmen would be finishing. Christie later confirmed he saw him talking to Jones.

On his arrival home that night Evans was met by Ethel in the hallway. She asked about Beryl and the baby, as she had not seen them during the day. He said that they had got up early to go on holiday to Bristol. Ethel no doubt was surprised, saying that Beryl had not mentioned any holiday to her.

Evans went on to say that Beryl would write to her. Later that evening he went to see his mother, Mrs Probert, telling her that Beryl and the baby had gone to stay with her father, William Thorley, in Brighton for a few days. His mother was surprised by this, as she had been under the impression that Beryl and her father did not have a close relationship. On his way back to Rillington Place Evans called into the Kensington Park Hotel for a much-needed drink. It must have been thirsty work telling all these lies.

We now move on to the next day, Thursday November 10 1949. Evans again went to work as usual. He was planning to ask his employer, Mr Alder, for an advance on his wages. Mr Alder told him that the arrangement was for his wife to collect £5 every Friday from his pay packet, and he would wait as usual until his wife collected the money the next day. Evans did not like this at all. He said he would leave if he did not get the advance on his wages, but it would seem that Mr Alder welcomed this. He hit back, telling Evans that he had just about had enough of him. He then paid him off and told him to collect his cards the next day.

When Evans arrived home he told the Christies that Beryl and the baby were now moving with him to Bristol, as he had been offered a better job there. He would therefore be vacating the flat. He asked Christie if he knew anyone who would buy his furniture, and Christie directed him to a Mr Hookway in Portobello Road. Evans made contact with Mr Hookway and it was arranged that the furniture dealer would call on Sunday November 13 to give him a price.

This of course meant Evans had to move the bodies of his wife and baby before then, but he understood the workmen would be finishing their work on Friday November 11, so his plan to put them into the wash-house would be able to go ahead.

Sometime between November 9 and 10 Evans paid a visit to Beryl's grandmother, Mrs Barnett, who lived in Ladbroke Grove, a short distance from Rillington Place. He told her that Beryl and the baby were in Scotland, which Mrs Barnett found very strange.

At this point I would like to comment on something I found rather odd. It was always said that Beryl's mother, Elizabeth Simmonds, had died, with no mention of when or how, yet here in Mrs Barnett's house at the time Evans visited we have a Miss Simmonds (Christian name not revealed) who claimed to be Mrs Barnett's daughter! Later Miss Simmonds confirmed to the police that she was present in the house at the time of Evans' visit.

Evans then went to see his mother, who had been constantly asking the whereabouts of Beryl and the baby. He told her that Beryl had written to him and in reply he had sent her 30 shillings. Now it was said that Evans could not read or write, so I would have thought Mrs Probert would have asked to see Beryl's letter (which of course did not exist). Again it must have been obvious to Mrs Probert that here were more of her son's lies. Surely if she was concerned, why did she not demand to see the letter?

We now move on to Friday November 11. The workmen had completed the work on the wash-house and left. The carpenter had also left, but was due back on Monday for a couple of hours to clean up, and would have no reason to go near the wash-house.

I believe Evans hid the bodies between the nights of Friday November 11 and Saturday the 12th. Under cover of darkness he dumped his wife's body under the wash-house sink, stacking the wood left by the workmen up against the sink in the hope that the body would not be seen. Baby Geraldine's body, still dressed, he placed behind the door, covering her with a few pieces of wood. There in that filthy wash-house the bodies remained for three weeks.

This callous man did not love his wife, or if he did it must have been short and sweet. In the case of his baby daughter I have no words to describe his action.

There has always been strong disagreement in this dreadful case about who murdered who. We can only come to our own conclusions as to what really happened. If Christie was the murderer, he would not have cared one way or the other about the victims' suffering as his whole life was made up of murder and perversion. The thought of the bodies of Beryl and baby Geraldine lying in that awful wash-house would not have bothered him at all.

If it was Evans who killed them, how could he have lived with himself knowing what he had done, and desecrated the bodies of his wife and child by dumping them in that wash-house? It was monstrous.

In fact I believe that one of these men murdered these two innocent victims, while the other helped to hide the bodies.

On Sunday November 13 Mr Hookway, the furniture dealer, arrived. Before paying Evans £40 for the lot, he asked if there was any outstanding debt on the furniture. Evans lied, saying there was none. On Monday the November 14 the furniture was taken away. The same day the carpenter finished his work and left.

Evans then proceeded to rip up Beryl's and the baby's clothes, which filled two sacks. Albert Rollings, a ragman, called to collect these - Evans took no money for them. In the afternoon he went to the cinema and then on to his favourite pub, the Kensington Park Hotel. Later he took the train to Cardiff and a local connection on to Merthyr Vale, where his aunt and uncle Mr and Mrs Lynch lived. He arrived at just after 6.30am on Wednesday November 15.

The Lynches were both very surprised to see their nephew at such an early hour and immediately asked where Beryl and the baby were. More lies - he told them they were staying with her father in Brighton. He then went on to say that he and his boss had come to Cardiff looking for further business, but the car had broken down and it could be a few days before it was repaired.

Those few days went into almost two weeks. Evans did the rounds of the local pubs with his uncle, borrowing money from him which he never paid back. While in Merthyr he sold Beryl's wedding ring and bought a new shirt. He had already bought a new camel coat with the money he had had from the sale of the furniture. For reasons unknown, he went back to 10 Rillington Place either on the November 22 or 23 to see Christie.

Now let us go back to the nights of Friday November 11 and 12, when Evans must have put the bodies in the wash-house. The question is - when did Christie get involved? I have no doubt he did get involved, but I do not believe he murdered them.

On the night of Tuesday November 8, when Evans murdered Beryl and the baby, I believe Christie may have gone upstairs and seen what Evans had done. Alternatively, Christie may have seen him carrying Beryl's body or the baby's to the wash-house.

If that is the case, why did Christie not go to the police? Was it because of the two bodies already buried in the garden, and his past criminal record? I do not believe he wanted to become involved in Evans' murders - he could have ended up back in prison.

We shall never know what took place between Evans and Christie on November 22 or 23. I believe Evans went back to Merthyr Vale knowing that Christie was not going to help him to remove the bodies from the wash-house and that he was bent on revenge towards Christie, as we will see from the second statement he made to the police at Merthyr Vale. I also believe Ethel Christie knew what was going on, but that she chose to protect Christie by standing back and say nothing.

When Evans arrived back at Merthyr Vale he told his aunt and uncle he had now left Beryl, as she was expecting a baby by another man. To say this of his dead wife shows again what a miserable creature he was. All his life he had managed to get out of difficult situations by telling lies. But he must have known by now that time was running out for him.

Mrs Lynch was appalled when Evans told her this story. She wrote to his mother, her sister, telling her that Evans had been staying with her since November 13 and what he had been saying to them. She feared he was telling more of his lies. Mrs Probert replied that she had not seen or heard of Beryl or the baby for three weeks. She told her sister she never wanted to see her son ever again, because of the lies he was telling and the people he owed money to and never paid back. She said he was no good, just like his father. She had to pay off the remaining debt on the furniture as she had stood guarantor.

When Mrs Lynch told Evans of his mother's letter he was furious, saying he had not sold the furniture and it was still in the flat at Rillington Place. He called his mother a liar and stormed out of the house. This seems to me very much like the pot calling the kettle black.

On Saturday November 26 Beryl's brother Basil Thorley, who was a projectionist at the local cinema in Notting Hill, discovered that Beryl and the baby were not with his father, William Thorley, in Brighton. He immediately told Mrs Probert. Evans' older sister Eileen went to see Christie. He was not at home, but Ethel spoke to her, saying that all they knew was what Evans had told them - Beryl and the baby had gone on holiday to Bristol and he was going to get a job there. Eileen told Ethel she was not telling her the truth, and with that remark Ethel closed the door.

Then Maureen, Evans' stepsister, went to 10 Rillington Place to question the Christies, as she was not satisfied with the response that Eileen had got from Ethel. Both John and Ethel were at home when she arrived. Christie repeated what Ethel had told her sister Eileen. She asked to see Evans' flat but was refused, Christie saying she would have to contact the agents for permission. She called them both bloody liars. With that Christie slammed the door, saying he did not have to listen to that kind of talk.

Chapter Four

LIES AND ACCUSATIONS

Evans by now must have been in a desperate state. He had no job, very little money and no permanent place to live. He was constantly being asked the whereabouts of Beryl and the baby. All this must have been wearing him down.

On the afternoon of the November 30 1949 Evans went to Merthyr Tydfil Police Station and asked to speak to an officer. He was seen by Detective Constable Evans, who told him to sit down and tell him the purpose of coming to the police station. Evans said he had disposed of his wife and put her body down a drain. The officer cautioned him but Evans continued, saying he couldn't sleep and wanted to get it off his chest.

The officer took him to the CID, where Evans made his first statement as follows:

Statement 1 at Merthyr (summary)

"At the beginning of October 1949 my wife Beryl told me she was expecting another baby, and she was three months gone. She was extremely upset over this as our daughter Geraldine was barely ten months old. I told her that she had had one and another wouldn't make any difference. She went on to say she was going to get rid of it, and later she bought a syringe and started to use it on herself, at the same time taking various tablets. It had no effect, except to make her look ill. I believe she went to see a woman who might abort her for £1.

"On Monday November 7 I went to work and after making a few deliveries I pulled up at a roadside café for something to eat. While I was there waiting for my breakfast a man started talking to me saying that I looked worried. I told him everything. He said "I can certainly help you with this" and he went outside and a few minutes later came back with a bottle. He told me to tell my wife to take it first thing in the morning, lie down on the bed for a few hours and that should do the job. He would not take any money and he wished me luck.

"When I arrived home in the evening my wife as usual started another row, but I took no notice of her. She asked for a cigarette and went to my overcoat pocket and found the bottle. I told her what it was for, but I said she should not take it and I would throw it away.

"The next day Tuesday November 8 when I got home from work there weren't any lights on in the flat. I put a penny in the gas meter and lit the gas light in the kitchen and then going into the bedroom, the baby was in the cot and my wife was lying on the bed. The bottle was on the pillow. I touched her and I could see she was dead. I fed the baby and when it was dark I carried my wife's body outside and lifted a drain cover up in front of the house and pushed her body inside."

Evans then signed this statement.

The Merthyr police telephoned Notting Hill Police Station and three officers were sent to raise the manhole cover outside 10 Rillington Place. It took all three to lift it, but they found nothing. When Evans was told of this, he repeated that he had put the body there. The police said he was not telling the truth. Evans then decided to change his story, saying that what he had told them was to protect a man named Christie. He said the story of meeting a man in a café was untrue, and said he would like to tell the true story.

Statement 2 at Merthyr (summary)

Evans then made another statement to Merthyr Police:

"Arriving home from work one evening, Christie met me in the hallway saying he would like a word regarding my wife Beryl. Christie said that Ethel and himself knew that Beryl was trying to end her unwanted pregnancy, if you both had come to me sooner I could have done this without any risk. He then showed me a medical book but I was none the wiser as I was unable to read. With the stuff he said he used 1 in 10 may die. I then told him no! and went upstairs. My wife started to talk about how Christie could help her and I said no! She flew into a temper and told me to mind my own business, she was going through with it.

"The next day Tuesday November 8 I went to work about 6.30am. Before leaving my wife said that all had been arranged with Christie to abort her that morning and would I tell Christie on my way out that everything was OK. When I got home that evening Christie met me in the hallway and said it did not work and Beryl had died. Followed by Christie I went into the bedroom and she was lying on the bed covered with the eiderdown, there was blood on her nose and mouth and she had been bleeding from her bottom part. Christie then said he would force open Mr Kitchener's flat door and put her body in there later and when it was dark he would put her body down the drain in front of the house.

"I said I would take the baby to my mother's, but Christie said it would look suspicious and that he knew a couple in Acton who would be happy to look after her. He told me to sell all the furniture and leave London as soon as possible.

"Friday November 11 I had no work to go to, as the previous day I had packed it in. So I went to see my mother to tell her that Beryl and the baby had gone to Brighton on holiday. When I got back to Rillington Place Christie said the couple from Acton had collected Geraldine. When the furniture had been taken I ripped up all Beryl's clothes and a rag dealer took two sacks full. Before taking the train to Cardiff I went to the pictures and had a drink at the Kensington Park Hotel. I arrived at Merthyr Vale at about 6.40am on Tuesday November 15."

Evans then signed the second statement.

As you will recall, when Evans left Christie on November 22 or 23 I believe he was bent on taking revenge on Christie for not helping him to remove the bodies from the wash-house. In his second statement he took that revenge by incriminating Christie.

In my view both statements are unbelievable. Evans claimed that Christie had performed an abortion on Beryl, looked at her dead body and the blood from her nose, mouth and bottom, yet showed no reaction. Then he claimed to have agreed to help Christie to put her body in Mr Kitchener's flat. He did all that Christie told him, allowed his baby daughter to be handed over to complete strangers, sold his furniture and high-tailed it to Merthyr Vale. Then he went on to tell a further pack of lies to his relatives about Beryl and the baby's whereabouts. This is a man who knew full well what he had done, yet he accused Christie of killing his wife and later his daughter.

I believe Christie had no motive to do this. True, he was also a murderer in the worst possible sense, but the severe bruises on Beryl's face were not his style. He had been married to Ethel for nearly 30 years and as far as we know he had never laid a finger on her. In contrast, it was well known that Evans had started hitting his own wife within a short time of their marriage.

When Evans' second statement was phoned through to Notting Hill Police, they went to see Mrs Probert to make further inquiries as to where Beryl and the baby could be. She told them she knew nothing. Mrs Probert was quite honest with the police, saying her son was a compulsive liar and always had been.

On December 1 the police went to search 10 Rillington Place. Christie showed them Evans' empty flat. In it the police found a briefcase which had been reported as stolen, along with newspaper cuttings of the Stanley Setty murder (Setty was a car dealer whose murder had recently been in the papers; his killer had dropped his dismembered body from a plane over the Essex marshes). They now decided that Evans should be brought back to London and questioned over the stolen briefcase. What they failed to do on this visit was to inspect the wash-house.

They interviewed both the Christies, who made no secret of the frequent rows between Evans and his wife and how Beryl was trying to end her unwanted pregnancy, which had made her look ill and haggard. Because of Mrs Probert's insistence to the police and the fact that the family had discovered that Beryl and the baby were not with her father in Brighton, the police decided that another search of 10 Rillington Place was vital.

After a further thorough search inside the house they went outside into the back garden. Christie was very uneasy, standing near the spot where he had buried the two bodies. The officers looked up and down the garden, which was extremely untidy, then one of the officers tried the wash-house door, which was jammed. Ethel promptly fetched a metal bar which they used to open it, saying it was always hung behind the back door for the tenants to use it.

The officer then opened the door. It was dark inside. He shone his torch on to the pile of wood stacked against the sink. When he removed this wood he was able to see a bundle wrapped in green cloth stuffed underneath. He pulled it out, and as he did so two human feet slid out. There was a gasp of horror from Ethel.

The officer went back inside and found the body of the baby behind the door, covered with a few pieces of wood, fully dressed and with a tie around her neck.

The bodies were quickly taken away. Beryl's father, William Thorley, who was living in Brighton at the time of her murder, had the agonising task of identifying them. At 2 pm the same day a Dr Teare started a post mortem. Earlier in the day Detective Inspector Black and Detective Sergeant Corfield had been sent to Merthyr to bring Evans back for questioning over the stolen briefcase.

Later the Notting Hill Police telephoned Merthyr, telling them that the bodies of Beryl and the baby had been found and that they were not to discuss anything with Evans on the journey back and should keep the media away from him.

When Evans arrived at Notting Hill Police Station he was seen by Chief Inspector Jennings in the presence of Inspector Black. Evans was shown a sash cord together with a green tablecloth, which had been used to wrap Beryl's body in. They also showed him Geraldine's clothes and the tie that had been found around her neck. Jennings went on to say that at 11.50am on Friday December 2 1949 they had found concealed in the wash-house at 10 Rillington Place the dead bodies of his wife Beryl Evans and daughter Geraldine. It was established in both cases that death was due to strangulation. "I believe you are responsible for their deaths," said the officer.

No doubt in a state of shock, all Evans was able to say was 'yes – yes'. He was then cautioned before making a statement as follows:

Evans' first statement At Notting Hill Police Station

"My wife was incurring debt after debt and I could not stand it any longer so I strangled her. I put her body in Mr Kitchener's flat then waited until it was dark and the Christies had gone to bed. I then put her under the sink in the wash-house."

Evans then signed it. He then went on to say that it was a great relief to have it all out in the open and he would to tell them what had led up to it all.

Evans' second statement At Notting Hill Police Station

"I worked for Lancaster Foods, but my wife was always moaning about the long hours I was away and she was left with the baby all the time and most of all the shortage of money. So I got another job at Continental Wine Stores, less hours and less money." (this did not make sense). "I had to borrow money £20 from my employer and later I was given the sack" (he doesn't say what for).

"I was out of work for three weeks and the rows with my wife got worse. I then went back to work for Lancaster Foods and it was arranged with my employer Mr Alder my wife would collect £5 of my wages every Friday." (why?) "I received a letter from J Brodericks the hire purchase company saying that the payments on the furniture were in arrears." (again his inability to read must be in question.) "When I showed the letter to my wife she admitted it was true, also we were in debt over the rent. I told her to stop squandering my money or I would leave her. She replied saying I could go any time and she would be rid of me. On Tuesday November 8 1949 when I got home from work we had a furious row. I could stand it no more and I strangled her.

"When it was dark and the Christies were in bed I took her body down to the wash-house and put it under the sink. On Wednesday November 9 1949 I got up and fed and changed my baby and put her back in the cot and went of to work.

"On Thursday November 10 1949 I fed and changed my baby and went to work, I tried to borrow money from my boss but he paid me off and told me to collect my cards the next day. When I got home I strangled my baby and later about midnight I put her body behind the door in the wash-house covering her with pieces of wood. I sold all the furniture to a Mr Hookway for £40 and left for Merthyr Vale and the rest you know."

Evans then signed the statement.

How can one believe what Evans says in his last statement? He strangles his wife, then leaves his baby alone all day in her cot the next day and the following day. He should have known that a baby will go on crying until someone picks it up. The Christies would have heard the continual crying, and one must wonder what state this poor little mite would have been in if what Evans said were true.

Evans went on to say that he came home and strangled her. I do not believe this. Everything he said was lies. You can catch a thief, but a liar is almost impossible.

When Evans attacked Beryl on that fatal night, she was four months pregnant and the post-mortem revealed she would have had a little boy. It also showed considerable bruising on her face and a series of abrasions on her throat. There was further bruising on the back of her neck and thighs. There was no evidence of an attempted abortion. The cause of death was asphyxia due to strangulation.

Baby Geraldine's post-mortem revealed that her face was badly swollen. The tie around her neck was extremely tight, causing severe bruising to the muscles around part of the voice box, and her stomach was empty. Cause of death was asphyxia due to strangulation.

We are led to believe that when Beryl's brother, Basil Thorley, was informed of her death and that of the baby, he said that Evans had probably killed them both. That comment makes it clear that Beryl had been complaining to her brother about the way Evans was treating her.

Chapter Five

EVANS IN THE DOCK

While awaiting his trial in Brixton Prison, Evans was seen by Dr J C Matheson, the Principal Medical Officer for the prison, on more than one occasion. Dr Matheson came to the conclusion that Evans was telling the truth when he said he had killed his wife and baby daughter. His impression of Evans was that he was an inadequate psychopath with schizoid traits.

Doctor Matheson described a psychopath as a person who always wants to get his own way and does not think of the consequences. This matches the behaviour of Evans in his childhood and thereafter.

The trial of Timothy John Evans opened in Court 1 at The Central Criminal Court at the Old Bailey on Wednesday January 11 1950. The presiding judge was Mr Justice Lewis. Leading the prosecution was Mr Christmas Humphreys, assisted by a Mr Elam. For the defence was Mr Malcolm Morris QC.

Evans was granted legal aid (his defence did not have the resources or funds to obtain all the information needed to help his client).

At that time the law in this country was that a person could only be tried for one murder at a time. For this reason Evans was charged only with the murder of his daughter Geraldine Evans on November 10 1949.

He pleaded not guilty. There would be little hope of mercy for a man who had murdered a defenceless baby in cold blood and without provocation.

Mr Christmas Humphreys opened the case for the prosecution by telling the jury of the full details of the unhappy marriage of the defendant and his wife. He went on to explain the reason why Evans may have gone to the police in Merthyr; because his lies were being exposed. Another possibility given was that he had gone in the hope that his daughter was safe with the couple in Acton whom Christie had given her to.

The prosecution told the jury that Evans was claiming that Christie had murdered Geraldine and also killed his wife Beryl in the process of performing an illegal abortion, but then later in a statement he had changed his story and confessed to the murders of both his wife and child, and stated how and when he had killed them. Concluding his speech, Mr Humphreys pointed out that Evans was being tried for the murder only of his daughter.

The defence for Evans was undertaken by a firm of solicitors, Freeborough, Slack & Co, who compiled a short summary which included interviews with Evans at Brixton Prison and the statements of several witnesses including the police. There were a total of 32 statements taken from 23 people including the workmen, but these were not given to the defence. There was no obligation for the prosecution to give them to the defence and they did not do so. However, they should have given the defence the names and addresses of these witnesses; by not doing so they failed in their duty.

It is not clear who Evans' solicitors interviewed, but it was not the workmen as it was not clear to them at the time how important that might have been. As the prosecution did not call most of these witnesses, the defence did not learn how important they might have been. It therefore cannot be said that Evans had a fair trial.

The summary for the defence had been handed to Mr Morris on January 4. He did everything for his client a barrister could possibly have done, but he had an extremely difficult case on his hands. His client had signed a confession saying he had killed his wife and daughter, then gone on to accuse another man of the crime. Evans' defence was that Christie had murdered both his wife and daughter. The reason for making this allegation was that when the police had informed him that his daughter Geraldine had been found dead in the wash-house at 10 Rillington Place he had believed she was still alive.

John and Ethel Christie in the back garden at 10 Rillington Place

Mrs Beryl Susanna Evans

The front of 10 Rillington Place

The back garden at 10 Rillington Place

Christie's kitchen at 10 Rillington Place

Christie's kitchen showing the alcove door open and the near-naked body of
Hectorina MacLennan

Ethel Christie's body under the floor boards can be seen wrapped in a blanket

The wash-house at 10 Rillington Place

Daily Mirror

WED APR. 1 1963

FORWARD WITH THE PEOPLE

1½

No. 15,359

Registered at G.P.O. as a Newspaper

QUEEN MARY

Today's issue records on other pages the memorable scenes in story and pictures of

The Last Farewell

CHRISTIE IS CHARGED WITH MURDER

JOHN REGINALD HALLIDAY CHRISTIE, 55, OF RILLINGTON-PLACE, NOTTING HILL, WEST LONDON, WAS CHARGED LAST NIGHT WITH THE MURDER OF HIS WIFE, MRS. ETHEL CHRISTIE, 54, WHOSE BODY WAS FOUND BURIED UNDER THE FLOORBOARDS AT NO. 10, RILLINGTON-PLACE, LAST WEDNESDAY.

Christie will appear at West London magistrates' court today.

By HOWARD JOHNSON

The man who recognised Christie at Putney—P.C. Thomas Ledger, 43.

JOHN REGINALD HALLIDAY CHRISTIE, heading down and holding his hat against his face, enters the Notting Hill, London, police station last night by a back door. He was later charged with the murder of his wife.

Christie being taken to the police station by PC Ledger who arrested him

Trinity Mirror/Mirrorpix/Alamy

killing Mrs. Evans, but at his own trial he said he had done so. When Evans stood in the dock Christie, upon whose own subsequent confession, had already strangled two other women.

No reliability can be placed on his words—but had it been known when Evans was tried that two skeletons already lay in the garden at Rillington-place it would assuredly have made an impact upon the jury.

Crime

THESE grave matters alone are enough to justify the request which the Evans family have now made for an inquiry into all the circumstances. This should at once be set on foot.

Another point of profound interest raised in the trial was that of the accused's state of mind. Of three expert witnesses, one said that he was not responsible for his actions, but the other two disagreed. The jury, by their verdict, said he knew what he was doing and knew it to be wrong.

In the eyes of the law, therefore, Christie is sane. There is not the slightest doubt, however, that he is grossly abnormal—and there are those who say that this should be enough to save him from the death penalty. Here we begin to tread upon shifting ground. At what point is abnormality so pronounced as to make a man not fully responsible for his actions?

Punishment

IT can be argued that every murderer is abnormal—at least at the moment when the crime is committed. But if that is admitted, and abnormality excuses murder, then murder would cease to be a punishable offence.

These are the vexed and disputable aspects which raise once more the whole question of the desirability, or otherwise, of capital punishment. It will be asked again whether there should be degrees of murder, as in America, or the admission, as in Scotland, of the doctrine of "diminished responsibility."

Christie's macabre career has come to an end—but the Christie case will echo down the corridors of Time.

BABY'S BOTTLE
Still half-full

First, there are the Evans family—his mother, Mrs. Probert, and his sister, Mrs. Eleanor Ashby, who live in St. Mark's-road, a few hundred yards from 10, Rillington - place, where Timothy Evans had a flat.

Mrs. Ashby said last night of her 25-year-old lorry - driver brother : " Tim did not know his baby was dead until he arrived at the police station in Notting Hill. He told me that after he was charged.

" We now know that when the police searched at Rillington-place they found all Geraldine's belongings hidden in a cupboard in Christie's front room.

" Her clothes, her pram, and even her feeding-bottle, half-filled with milk, were there. No one has mentioned these facts before."

DEVOTED
To his daughter

Now for Evans' aunt — Mrs. Violet Lynch, of Mount Pleasant, near Merthyr Tydfil. He went to her home after leaving Rillington-place. Of those days she said : " His life was devoted to Geraldine and he would not have harmed a hair on her head.

" When on trial Timmy swore to me over and over again that a man named Christie had promised to take the child to a safe home.

" What a terrible man he was to have sat there after murdering Beryl, Timmy's wife, and yet saying nothing as he watched Timmy being sent to the gallows."

There will also be before the Home Secretary the report of the Evans trial, where it was first alleged that Christie knew something about the deaths of Mrs. Evans and the baby.

Then there are Christie's admissions at his own trial, and the questioning there of Chief Inspector Albert Griffin.

Sir Lionel Heald, the Attorney-General asked the inspector : Have you any ground for believing that the wrong man was hanged in the Evans case ?

Inspector Griffin : None.

TWO MEN ?
' It is possible '

Sir Lionel : " Is one possibility that two men were concerned with the death of Mrs. Evans ? "

Inspector Griffin : " It is possible. I do not know."

And, yesterday, the judge said of the Evans murder : " It is foolish for us to pretend it may not be a matter of disturbing interest."

There is, too, the view of the Home Secretary at the time, Mr. Chuter Ede. He said last night : " I am making no comment on this matter."

Whether more is heard of it rests with his successor, Sir David Maxwell Fyfe, who will have before him today these final words from the Penal Reform League : " It is imperative that public confidence in justice be maintained."

THIS is a report of the Old Bailey trial of Timothy John Evans, who was sentenced to death on Friday the 13th of January 1950, for the murder of his 14 - month - old daughter, Geraldine :

The prosecution said that the strangled bodies of Evans's 20-year-old wife, Beryl Susanna, and his daughter were found by the police on December 2, 1949, wrapped up in parcels in a wash-house at his home at 10, Rillington-place, Notting Hill.

Evans, who said he could not read or write, repeated the oath after the court usher when he went into the witness-box.

No idea

He denied in evidence being responsible for the death of either his wife or child.

He alleged that John Reginald Halliday Christie, who lived in another flat in the house, said he was going to treat his wife to end her pregnancy. When Evans returned from work on November 8 Christie told him he had some bad news—Mrs. Evans was dead.

While Evans was feeding the baby he heard Christie coughing and blowing on the stairs.

On going out, Evans said he saw him trying to get the body of Mrs. Evans down the stairs.

He added : " I helped Christie to carry my wife's body to the empty flat and never saw it again."

He also said Christie told him he would make arrangements with friends to look after the baby.

On November 10, on returning home from work. Evans said he was informed that the child had been collected by those friends.

Later, said Evans, he went to stay with relatives in Wales, as he told them his wife and baby were staying with other relatives.

All untrue

Evans also said that he had no idea his daughter had been strangled until told by the police.

He was asked why he told police at Merthyr Tydfil—when he gave himself up—that he had disposed of his wife's body in a drain. He said that was not true but was said to " protect Christie.

Replying to Mr. Christmas Humphreys (prosecuting) Evans admitted he made five different statements confessing to the murder of his wife and child. But he declared they were untrue.

Evidence was called of statements alleged to have been made by Evans telling of repeated nagging by his wife which ended in his strangling her.

The prosecution also alleged that Evans sold his wife's wedding ring for six shillings to a South Wales jeweller, and later disposed of her furniture.

Christie, in the witness-box, denied any knowledge of the death of either Evans's wife or child. He also denied he disposed of their bodies.

' A lie '

Mr. Malcolm Morris (defending) : I have to suggest to you that you are responsible for the death of Mrs. Evans and little girl or if that isn't so, at least you knew much more about these deaths than you have said ?

Christie : That is a lie.

He also denied that, after learning Mrs. Evans was pregnant he told her husband that could relieve her of her condition without any risk. He advised her not to take pills she was using.

Medical evidence was given which established that Mrs. Evans died from strangulation and there was no sign of interference to end her pregnancy.

Summing up. Mr. Justice L[...]

THE EVANS BABY
—GERALDINE.

Turn to Page 2, Col.

THE AMAZING CHRISTIE STORY—PAGE THREE

Baby Geraldine Evans, pictured in a press cutting at the time

Mr Humphrey's first witness for the prosecution was Dr Teare, who confirmed that there was no attempted abortion on Mrs Beryl Evans and that the cause of her death was asphyxia due to strangulation.

John Christie was then questioned by Mr Christmas Humphreys for the prosecution. Christie gave his evidence about the Evans' unhappy marriage and suggested that Evans was extremely violent towards his wife, as she had on many occasions complained to him and his wife Ethel, saying that she wanted a separation from Evans.

Christie was then cross-examined by Malcolm Morris, who suggested that Christie might have attempted to abort Mrs Evans, but she had started to panic and he had strangled her. He went on to expose Christie's past criminal record. Then he came straight to the point, saying he was suggesting that Christie was responsible for the deaths of both Mrs Evans and her daughter Geraldine.

Christie was outraged. "That is a lie!" he shouted. At this point he showed signs of feeling unwell and was asked by the Mr Justice Lewis if it would help if he was allowed to sit down. Christie thanked him and said it would.

Mr Morris continued to remind Christie of the allegation in one of Evans' statements that Christie had murdered Beryl and Geraldine.

In Mr Humphrey's re-examination he quickly had to make good the damage that had been done by the revelations of Christie's past criminal record. He first asked Christie what he had been doing in the First World War - fighting for his country no doubt, and blinded by mustard gas. He reminded him that when he had finished his Army service in 1919 he had been given a small disability pension. Then during World War II he had been a special constable, helping the victims of the Blitz, and had quite rightly been commended for all his good work.

Evans was a pathetic witness, to think he could have been clever enough to have thought out a scheme to accuse Christie of these murders, as his second statement suggested. When asked what motive Christie might have had to commit this crime, the answer Evans gave to the court was: "Well, he was home all day."

Then Evans was examined by his own counsel, Malcolm Morris. Mr Morris reminded Evans of the first statement he had made at Merthyr Vale, which Evans said was not true, and that it had been made up to protect Christie. He then went on to explain how Christie had become involved in the death of his wife in the attempt to abort her and to arrange for his baby to be looked after by a young couple he knew in Acton. Christie had told him that he had been training to become a doctor and had produced a medical book for him to look at. Evans said he had been none the wiser, as he was unable to read. This seems to have been a repetition of Evans' second statement at Merthyr Vale.

In Christmas Humphreys' cross-examination Evans became very confused by the questions being put to him, which caused him to give answers that did not help his defence. In short, he made a hopeless mess of trying to defend himself.

Christmas Humphreys asked Evans why, when Inspector Jennings had told him that the bodies of his wife and daughter had been found and he had reason to believe he was responsible for their deaths, he had replied 'Yes'. Evans replied 'I was upset when he told me my daughter was dead'.

Later on Evans said that because his daughter was now dead he had nothing else to live for. Further on in his trial he was asked by the prosecution if he had anything to live for now. He replied: "Yes sir, I have got a lot of things to live for."

Christmas Humphreys asked Evans if he was trying to tell the court that he had gone to the police and confessed to a murder because he was worried about his daughter. Then Malcolm Morris stood up, saying there had been no confession of murder - all the defendant had said was that he had disposed of his wife and put her down a drain at 10 Rillington Place.

Judge Justice Lewis said: "It sounds very much like murder to me."

Christmas Humphreys then said to Evans: "You went to the police and described in great detail how you murdered your wife and child. This was said to protect the man who you say committed these murders. Is that correct?"

"Yes" said Evans. "Why?" asked Humphreys.

As the cross-examination went on, Evans was forced to admit lie after lie. Christmas Humphreys put the question to Evans: "Am I correct in saying that you are prepared to lie or tell the truth when it suits you?"

"I am not lying, my life is at stake here" said Evans.

"When you made the confession to the police you said to them that it was such a relief to get it off your chest and have it out in the open, did you say that?"

"Yes, but it was a load of lies."

"So you are saying it was a relief to get all these lies off your chest?"

"I was upset" said Evans.

Judge Justice Lewis then said to Evans: "Will you answer the question that is being put to you? Was this a relief for you to tell more lies?"

"I had no relief at all" said Evans.

"Will you listen to the questions you are asked?" replied the judge.

Christmas Humphreys' final question to Evans was if he could tell the court what Christie's motive could have been for strangling Beryl Evans, other than his earlier words, "Well he was home all day". Evans said he could not.

In his closing speech, Christmas Humphreys said it was an exceptional case. The jury had to consider the attack made by the defendant on Christie - was there a word of truth in it, taking into consideration Christie's disability at that time, did they believe Christie could have done it, and if he wanted to, why?

In his speech for the defence Malcolm Morris complained to the court that some witnesses had not been called to give evidence which might have helped Evans case. Morris perhaps knew he was fighting a losing battle. The case against Evan's was overwhelming, but he did a fine job defending his client. His last effort was to warn the jury about Christie, as to whether he had been telling the truth.

In his summing up, Mr Justice Lewis reminded the jury that by law no one could be found guilty on suspicion alone, and the prosecution must prove it beyond all reasonable doubt. The judge heaped ridicule on Evans' first statement about meeting a man in a café and being given a bottle which would cause his wife to have a miscarriage. He went on talk about Evans' constant lies and said the statements he had made were outrageous. He went into full details of this confusing case.

Sadly Mr Justice Lewis had conducted his last trial. He was in failing health, and he died a few days after it had ended.

The jury took only 35 minutes to find Evans guilty. He was sentenced to death.

To the bitter end, his mother and his two sisters Eileen and Maureen fought non-stop to save him. Evans went on to protest his innocence to his mother and all his family, and continued to accuse Christie of killing Beryl and baby Geraldine. His family managed to arrange an appeal, but it failed. His Catholic priest heard his last confession, and what took place between them will never be known. Timothy John Evans was hanged on March 9 1950 and buried in the prison grounds.

If Evans had been tried for the murder of his wife instead of his daughter, and it had been proven that he was under strong provocation at the time, it is quite possible that he might not have been hanged. He might have been given a prison sentence instead. After the disclosures of the Christie murders a few years later, there would have been a public outcry for him to be pardoned.

Many have said, including some Members of Parliament, that Evans did not have a fair trial. Mr Justice Lewis, the presiding judge, was in very poor health and at times he seemed to lose patience with Evans, constantly telling him to answer the questions that were being put to him and not to wander off into another story. He also prompted his defence, Malcolm

Morris, telling him to stop rambling on and get to the point he was trying to make.

Chapter Six

THE KILLING STARTS AGAIN

After Evans' trial the Christies went to stay with Ethel's relatives in Sheffield for a holiday and to get away from it all. When they returned to Rillington Place, Christie's health was beginning to fail. He was losing weight and unable to sleep. Worst of all, thanks to the revelations brought out at the Evans trial, he lost his job at the post office. His doctor gave him a sick note for four weeks, but he was out of work for much longer.

In the summer of 1950 10 Rillington Place was put up for sale at the asking price of £1,500. A Mr McNeil viewed the property, and while he was there Christie asked him if he knew what had happened in this house, and if he believed in ghosts. McNeil told Christie that he was an undertaker and that sort of thing did not worry him. He was going to give it a good makeover.

It was obvious that Christie was worried about the two bodies buried in the garden. Fortunately for Christie, McNeil's surveyor's report was not good. The house was decaying, filthy and infested with vermin, and he advised his client not to buy it.

Later the house was bought by a Jamaican named Charles Brown, who by all accounts did not care what state the house was in. He went on to rent out all the rooms to black tenants. The Christies were horrified, but could do nothing about it. Christie eventually found a new job as a clerk with British Road Services, and his health for the time being improved. Their home life at 10 Rillington Place was however fraught with problems. Trouble with the new tenants increased and Ethel took one of them to court, saying she had been assaulted.

Christie's health once more began to go downhill and he was a patient for three weeks at St Charles Hospital. From there he was sent to Springfield Mental Hospital. When he eventually returned home it was clear to Ethel that he had become a very disturbed person. He left his job at British Road Services and became more agitated.

On December 14 1952 he strangled Ethel while she was in bed. Later he claimed that she had died from an overdose, but this was contradicted by her post-mortem; death was due to strangulation.

Christie then buried his wife's body under his front-room floorboards and set about concealing her death. He told relatives that she was unable to write to them because she had rheumatism in both hands, and she would visit them when she was feeling better. He told neighbours that she had gone on one of her visits to Sheffield, where later he would be joining her to start a new job. He showed Mrs Swan, his next door neighbour, a bogus telegram purporting to be from Ethel and saying she had arrived safely in Sheffield.

Christie would later say that Ethel had to go. He had been kept in check by her presence for more than 10 years, and now he was free he could fulfil all his sexual urges and needs - which he did.

In January 1953 he met Kathleen Maloney, a prostitute, in a café. He said she had followed him home, demanding 30 shillings and saying that if he did not give her the money she would say he had tried to interfere with her. Christie said he found her repulsive, drunk and unclean. He said that when they reached Rillington Place she had forced her way into his flat and had started to undress in the kitchen. There had been a struggle and she had attempted to hit him with a frying pan.

Christie told the police: "If anyone deserved to die, she did." He said she had been so drunk that she had fallen into a broken-down deckchair.

Christie lost no time. He strangled Kathleen and wrapped her body in a filthy blanket. He did not tell anyone whether he had sex with her or not. He put her body into an alcove in the kitchen.

Christie said that in February 1953 he had met another prostitute, again in a café; Rita Nelson. She was six months pregnant and looking for somewhere to live, which pleased Christie. He told her he would be leaving his own flat soon and she was more then welcome to come and take a look at it with him at 10 Rillington Place.

When they arrived, Rita suggested they start by living together, but the last thing Christie wanted was a long-term relationship with a woman, particularly one who was six months pregnant. That was not what he had brought her there for. They had intercourse, and then Christie without any effort pushed her into the notorious deckchair and gassed her. Rita was so drunk that she was unable to defend herself. She joined Kathleen Maloney in the kitchen alcove.

Some time in March 1953 Christie met Hectorina MacLennan, again a prostitute who was suppose to be living with her aunt in Putney. She however told Christie that she was living with a male friend named Baker and that they were having to leave their lodgings immediately for not paying their rent, so they were looking for somewhere to live. Christie invited the couple to stay at his flat until such time as they could find a place.

On arrival at 10 Rillington Place he gave them tea in the kitchen. The woman slept in the 'strangler's' deckchair while Christie slept on the floor in the kitchen. Baker slept in Christie's bedroom. He was keeping them apart to prevent them from having sex in his flat.

Christie disliked Baker and after a few days Christie told him to leave. This was obviously because he wanted to be left alone with Hectorina to carry out his murderous routine once again. However, Hectorina left with Mr Baker.

Later that night, to Christie's delight, Hectorina returned, saying she had no place to go and asking if she could stay with him for a few more days. As always he made his victim a cup of tea. His murderous plans were set in motion.

Then, for some unknown reason, Hectorina began to feel uneasy in Christie's presence. She told him she was leaving, but when she attempted to go he caught hold of her around the neck and dragged her to the floor, stripping off some of her clothes. He then had intercourse with her, during which he strangled her. She was dumped almost naked with the other bodies in the now-stinking alcove. At some time after putting his last victim into the alcove, Christie used wallpaper to cover its door over.

The next day Baker turned up, asking Christie if he had seen Hectorina. Christie denied all knowledge of her coming back to Rillington Place and invited Baker to help him find her.

It has been said that Christie was a necrophiliac, and it is quite possible he did indeed have further sex with his victims after he had killed them. He openly admitted that the dead bodies of women gave him a sense of peace and satisfaction because he was able to possess them completely.

Christie soon became short of money, so he decided to sub-let his flat, complete with his collection of corpses. He knew a Mr and Mrs Reilly who were looking for accommodation to rent, and offered them the flat. After viewing, Mr and Mrs Reilly paid him £7 13s rent in advance.

Christie now went on to make arrangements with Mr Hookway, the furniture dealer, to call and give him a price for the furniture. Mr Hookway's offer was somewhere in the region of £10. Christie wanted more, but Mr Hookway told him to take it or leave it. Christie reluctantly accepted this, and then asked him if he was including the mattress in the price. Mr Hookway responded: "That filthy mattress will probably walk out on its own!"

Christie then left 10 Rillington Place for the last time, and Mr and Mrs Reilly immediately moved in.

The day after they had moved in, the owner, Charles Brown, called to collect the weekly rent from all the tenants. He was taken aback to find that Christie had sub-let his flat and charged Mr and Mrs Reilly £7 13s in advance rent. He gave them 24 hours to vacate the premises.

On March 24 1953 a Mr Beresford Brown, who was living in the flat previously occupied by the Evans family, was given permission by the owner to use Christie's kitchen. His delight was short lived. When he attempted to put up a shelf on the wall at the back of the kitchen, it fell to the floor.

On closer examination he found the wall was hollow. He had discovered Christie's alcove.

Mr Brown ripped off the wallpaper and saw that behind it was some kind of enclosure. Part of the wood at the top was missing, and he was able to look through it, but he could see nothing.

He then went to find a torch and shone it through the gap. To his horror he saw what appeared to be the almost naked body of a woman. He called another tenant, a Mr Ivan Williams, to confirm exactly what he had seen.

The police were then called, and 10 Rillington Place was sealed off. The first body to be taken from the kitchen alcove was the one Mr Brown had discovered, that of Hectorina MacLennan. The scratches on her back and buttocks indicated that she had been dragged across the floor.

Rita Nelson and Kathleen Maloney were then pulled out; they had been propped up feet first against the alcove wall. The bodies were all taken to Kensington Mortuary.

All three victims in the alcove had no knickers on and semen was found in all their bodies. Carbon monoxide was found to be present in Hectorina Maclennan's blood. She had been dead for about four weeks.

In the case of Kathleen Maloney, alcohol was present in her blood. Due to advanced decomposition – she had been dead for about nine weeks - all that could be seen was the marks on her neck. Rita Nelson was found to be six months pregnant, and she had been dead for about ten weeks.

Mrs Christie's body was discovered under the front room floor boards. She had been dead for about thirteen weeks.

After a full search of the garden, the police found the remains of Ruth Fuerst and Muriel Eady. There was an old dustbin which apparently had been used as an incinerator. They also found a tin containing human pubic hair.

The police then began a thorough search for Christie, and his picture was on the front pages of many newspapers. There were many unconfirmed sightings, but most of them turned out to be a waste of police time.

He was eventually found on March 31 1953 by a PC Thomas Ledger on Putney Embankment. He was unkempt, unshaven, dirty and penniless, and strangely enough a newspaper cutting of Evans' trial was found on him. He was taken to Putney Police Station.

On the same day, in the presence of Chief Inspector Griffin and Detective Inspector Kelly, Christie made his first statement. He said killing his wife Ethel had been an act of mercy. She had been convulsive and unable to breath, which had upset him, so he had had no choice but to put her out of her suffering. Keeping her body under the floorboards meant they would still be together as they had always been, and it was a great comfort to him knowing that she was nearby.

He called the prostitute Kathleen Maloney a drunken slut who had attempted to hit him with a frying pan. He had got her on the deckchair and strangled her. He said Rita Nelson would not leave his flat and became violent, so he had knocked her to the floor and strangled her.

Hectorina MacLennan had forced her way into the flat and would not leave, and had started to lash out at him, so he had pushed her on to the deckchair and strangled her. As with Evans, all Christie's statements were different, and all were filled with lies.

After these murders Christie went on living at 10 Rillington Place for some time, eating his meals in the kitchen a few feet away from where his rotting victims were lying. He truly was a monster.

The other tenants said that Christie continued to put down Jeyes Fluid disinfectant in the hallway. It was obvious from this that a smell must have been coming from the kitchen alcove and the front room where Ethel's body lay under the floorboards.

In April 1953, while Christie was in prison awaiting trial, a Dr J A Hobson, a consultant physician in psychological medicine, interviewed Christie. Christie told Dr Hobson that he had killed Mrs Evans and that intercourse had taken place. He also claimed he had taken a clump of pubic hair from her. This prompted Christie's solicitors to ask for Beryl Evans' body to be exhumed to find out if hair had indeed been taken from her body. If this was the case, it would help to prove that Christie was insane.

The exhumation was carried out on May 18 1953. There was no sign of any pubic hair having been cut, and no evidence of semen in her body. When Christie was told of these findings he changed his story, saying the pubic hair he had collected and put in a tin box was from the three women he had put in the alcove.

While Christie was in Brixton Prison he put on weight and his health improved. Prison officers said he was very meticulous.

He was often asked by his fellow prisoners if he had really murdered all these women. Sometimes he would say he had, while at other times he would say deny it. He told filthy stories which revealed his hatred of women. He would go on to boast that he would not be hanged because he would be found insane. Broadmoor Prison would be his choice to serve out whatever sentence he was given, as he had heard it was very pleasant there.

Chapter Seven

THE TRIAL OF JOHN CHRISTIE

The trial of John Reginald Halliday Christie opened at The Central Criminal Court at The Old Bailey on Monday June 22 1953. The judge was Mr Justice Finnemore. Counsel for the Crown was Sir Lionel Heald QC, and counsel for the defence was Mr Derek Curtis-Bennett QC. Christie was charged with the murder of his wife Ethel Christie in December 1952. He pleaded not guilty.

Christie's legal expenses were paid by the Sunday Pictorial in return for the full rights to his story. There was of course wide speculation at the time of Christie's trial that Evans had been hanged when in fact he was innocent. All the morning and evening newspapers reported on the trial every day.

Christie admitted to killing his wife, but his counsel asked the jury to find that he was guilty but insane. Mrs Swan, the Christies' next-door neighbour, was one of the first witnesses to be questioned by the Attorney General. Her evidence was that she had last seen Mrs Christie some time between December 6 and December 10 1952. She said that on December 19, while she had been in her garden, Christie had come out and waved a piece of paper saying it was a telegram from Ethel to say that she had arrived safely in Sheffield.

The next witness, an employee of Maxwell Laundries, said Mrs Christie had been a regular customer. She had failed to collect some laundry that she had left with them on Friday December 12.

The next witness was Charles Brown, who confirmed to Mr Seaton for the Prosecution that he was the owner of 10 Rillington Place, which he had purchased on August 3 1950. He had let all the rooms. Mr and Mrs Christie already occupied the ground floor flat and about March 19 he had gone there to collect the rents due. He had found that Christie had sub-let his flat to a Mr and Mrs Reilly, and had immediately told the Reillys that they had to vacant the premises.

Ethel's brother, Henry Simpson Waddington, was called next by the Attorney General to give evidence in respect of his late sister. He said that Christie had written on Ethel's behalf to say that she had rheumatism in her hands and that he would be writing the letters for her until Ethel was able to write again. He also confirmed that Ethel made regular visits to Sheffield to see them, and Ethel never missed sending them a Christmas card. However, the last one, at Christmas 1952, had been signed by Christie, with a note saying not to worry about Ethel, he was going to cook Christmas dinner for her.

On March 24 1953 Mr Waddington identified the body of his late sister. A Mrs Judith Green, who worked in a jewellery shop, was then questioned by the Attorney General. She identified the man in the dock as the man who had come to the shop offering for sale a gold wrist watch and a wedding ring. On completion of the sale he had signed the shop ticket in the name of J R Christie. These pieces of jewellery were later identified as having belonged to Christie's late wife.

A Mr Frederic Snow, the Manager of the Penny Bank, Sheffield, was then examined by the Attorney General. He said that he had received a letter from Mrs Christie saying she wished to close her account, which had a balance of £10 15s 2d. The signature on the letter was compared to the specimen signature and he had had no reason to believe it was not genuine. Accordingly the money was sent to Mrs Christie at 10 Rillington Place by registered post.

For the prosecution, Mr Maxwell Turner examined Mrs Lena Louise Brown, the wife of Mr Beresford Brown, who had discovered the three bodies of the prostitutes in the Kitchen alcove. The last time she had seen Mrs Christie had been about eight days before her baby was born on December 18 1952. When she came home from hospital she noticed that

Mr Christie was constantly using disinfectant in the hallway, back yard and the front of the house. She asked Christie why he was using it on the front of the house, and he said it was because of dog fouling.

Mr Maxwell Turner, for the prosecution, examined Mr Franklin James Stewart, a former tenant at 10 Rillington Place. Mr Stewart said that the last time he had seen Mrs Christie had been shortly before Christmas, and she had been in perfect health at that time.

He added: "In February 1953, because I had not seen her, I asked Mr Christie if she was sick. He replied that she had gone to his sister for a break and was coming home the following week. I did notice a strong smell of Jeyes fluid in the hallway and I also saw him putting some down the drain pipe at the back of the house.

Mr Curtis-Bennett, cross-examining, said to Mr Stewart: "While you were living at 10 Rillington Place seven black tenants were living in one room and up to three in the other rooms. Is this correct?

"Yes."

"Did these people spill water in the hallway?"

"I do not know that."

"You were of course aware of the dirt these tenants left constantly in the hallway, and that therefore Mr Christie had no choice but to clean the hallway with disinfectant on a daily basis?" To this there was no answer.

Mrs Mary Margaret Reilly, examined by the Attorney General, confirmed that she had been looking for a place to rent and Mr Christie had made contact with her and made arrangements with her and her husband to view his flat. All his furniture had gone. Her husband had paid Mr Christie £7 13s in advance rent and they had moved in on March 23 1953.

Harold Henry Cooper, examined by The Attorney General, said that on the March 20 1953 Christie had arrived at Rowton House (a London 'doss house') and booked in for seven nights. He gave him a ticket to establish he had paid for those nights.

Police Constable Thomas Ledger, stationed at Putney Police Station, said that on March 31 he had come across a man on the Putney embankment. He had asked him for identity, which he was unable to give. He had asked him to remove his hat, at which he had recognised the man as John Reginald Halliday Christie.

Chief Inspector Albert Griffin of F Division, Hammersmith Police Station, had interviewed Christie on March 24 with Inspector Kelly at Putney Police Station. He had told Christie that the body of his wife had been found under the floorboards in the front room at 10 Rillington Place. Christie had then made his first statement.

Albert Griffin, Chief Inspector at F Division, was then cross-examined by Mr Curtis-Bennett, who went into great detail about the life of Christie and his past crimes.

On the second day of the trial Albert Griffin was recalled and the cross-examination by Mr Curtis-Bennett was continued. Reference was now made to the late Timothy John Evans and whether he had killed his wife Beryl and their daughter Geraldine.

Mr Curtis-Bennett, in his opening speech for the defence, said: "Your Lordship and members of the jury, when you have heard all the evidence of this case it is hoped that you will return the verdict of guilty but insane. It is also important that the issue of this case should be kept to. The accused has had frequent periods of insanity. This takes the form of killing a woman without a sexual motive. This is clearly evident in the case of Mrs Christie.

"I now refer to Christie's GP, Dr Odess, who gave evidence that Christie has been in bad health since 1944, has been constantly on drugs and was never examined by him for insanity, but he firmly believed he could be a mental case. In 1952 he eventually became a patient at Springfield Mental Hospital. When he killed his wife on December 14 1952 the state of Christie's mind at that time must be in question.

"I now come to the issue of the Timothy John Evans case. At this trial we are not concerned as to whether there was any miscarriage of justice or not."

Christie was then called into the witness box to take the oath and tell his horrific story to persuade the court he was insane. He was then examined by Mr Curtis-Bennett for the defence.

"In 1906 your grandfather died and were you taken to see him laid out in his coffin?

"Yes."

"You were at the tender age of eight years old?"

"Yes."

"Did this have any effect on you?"

"I do not think so but I can't be sure."

"Were you called up in April 1917 for the Army?"

"Yes."

"And while in France you were injured by a mustard gas explosion?"

"Yes."

"Following this you were blind for about five and half months?"

"Yes, I think that is correct."

"You said you were unable to speak for about three and half years?"

"I believe that is right."

"In 1920 you married Ethel Simpson Waddington?"

"Yes."

"Did you have any children during this marriage?"

"No."

"Because of your crimes of stealing, malicious wounding and consequently having to serve a prison sentence for these crimes your wife Ethel left you?"

"Yes."

"In 1933 while you were in prison Ethel paid you a visit and you begged her to come back to you, is that correct?"

"Yes."

"From then onwards you both seem to be very happy? Answer yes or no."

"Yes."

"Is it true that you kept a box of pubic hairs?"

"Yes."

"Did one of the sets belong to your wife?"

"I think so."

"Is it true that you became friendly with a Muriel Eady and a Ruth Fuerst, whom you took to 10 Rillington Place while your wife Ethel was away in Sheffield?"

"Yes."

"What happened on their visits to your flat?"

"I'm not sure."

"Do you remember if you used the gas on Miss Eady or Miss Fuerst or both?"

"I have an idea I used it on one of them."

"What did you do then?"

"I think I must have strangled them, I can't remember."

"How did you dispose of their bodies?"

"I believe I put them into the wash-house first and later I dug a hole in the garden and buried them."

"Can you tell the court if you have killed any more women?"

"I don't know, I may have done, sometimes I get things in my mind and cannot get them out."

"Was this before 1943?"

"It may have been."

"Before or after World War II?"

"I think so."

"Let us go on to 1949. Were you and your wife Ethel living in the ground floor flat at 10 Rillington Place?"

"Yes."

"Was there a Mr Kitchener, a retired railway man, living on the first floor, who was not in good health and waiting to go into hospital for an operation?"

"Yes."

"On the top floor was there a Mr and Mrs Evans together with their daughter Geraldine?"

"Yes."

"How well did you know this couple?"

"Not very well at first."

"Were they happy or not?"

"I think so."

"Was there trouble over a Lucy Endecott?"

"Yes."

"Was Mrs Evans pregnant, and did you know this?"

"Yes."

"Was she happy about her pregnancy?"

"Absolutely not, my wife Ethel and I were aware she was taking various steps to end her unwanted pregnancy, we both tried to advise her whatever she was doing to end this unwanted pregnancy was dangerous and she should stop it."

"Did you try and abort Mrs Evans?"

"Certainly not."

"Did you see her on Monday November 7 1949?"

"Yes, I think I went upstairs and found her lying on her kitchen floor unconscious. There was a strong smell of gas and I immediately opened her window. When Beryl recovered I gave her a glass of water. She asked me not to say anything about this."

"The next day, Tuesday November 8, was Evans out at work during the daytime?"

"Yes."

"Did you see Mrs Evans that day?"

"Yes."

"Did you go upstairs to see her?"

"Yes, she told me she was fed up with the life she had and that she had started yesterday to try and kill herself. She had intended to go through with it, and she asked further for my help to succeed in this. So I did."

Judge Justice Finnemore then addressed Christie.

"You say "So I did." What did you do?"

"She got a cover and laid down on the kitchen floor, saying she would do anything if I would help her."

"Did she mean, to kill her?"

"Yes."

"Did she mean you could have sex with her?"

"I think you could say that."

"Did you have sex with Mrs Evans?"

"Definitely not, I did try but due to the severe pain in my back I could not bend."

"What did you do next?"

"While she was laid down I got a piece of gas tubing and attached it to the gas point by the side of the fire place, this was used for the gas stove, then I put the gas tube to her face. When she was unconscious I think I strangled her with her stocking."

Mr Curtis-Bennett's examination then resumed.

"Then what did you do?"

"I left her there."

"When Evans came home from work, what did you say to him?"

"I told him that his wife had committed suicide."

"Did you say any more?"

"I told him that it was going to look very serious for him because of all the frequent rows between them both."

"Did you then go upstairs with Evans?"

"Yes."

"What took place then?"

"Evans saw his wife on the kitchen floor. He picked her up and carried her into the bedroom and covered her over with the eiderdown."

"We understand she was later found wrapped up in a green cloth and stuffed under the sink in the wash-house. What do you know of this?"

"I know nothing about this at all."

"At Evans' trial, did Mr Malcolm Morris for the defence suggest that you were responsible for the deaths of Mrs Evans and baby Geraldine?"

"Yes.

"But you denied it?"

"Yes."

"Then you had better tell us why you lied about not killing Mrs Evans."

"Because they accused me of killing them both."

Judge Justice Finnemore: "When you were in the witness box at Evans' trial, you were asked whether you had taken part in the of killing of Mrs Evans and her baby daughter and you denied it?"

"Yes"

"But why did you deny it?"

"It's been a very long time since then and I do not remember but I believe it was because I never touched the baby."

"What about Mrs Evans?"

"At that time I was accused of killing them both."

Examination continued: The question that Mr Malcolm Morris put to you at Evans trial was, "I am suggesting you are responsible for the deaths of Mrs Evans and her baby daughter". If this is not the case then you know much more about their deaths then you are saying and you were also of the opinion that Evans had killed his daughter?"

"Yes."

Judge Justice Finnemore then asked: "You say that you killed Mrs Evans and arranged with her husband for how her body would be disposed of and telling Evans how much trouble he was in, are you saying that you are unable to remember all this?"

"Yes sir, I just can't remember."

Examination continued. "When Mr Charles Brown purchased 10 Rillington Place in August 1950, do you agree that there was a change of residents at 10 Rillington Place?"

"Yes."

"What changes took place?"

"In all the rooms upstairs he rented them out to coloured people with white girls who were prostitutes. It was extremely upsetting."

"Was your wife upset?"

"Yes, my wife Ethel was assaulted by some of these tenants, and took them to court."

"Is it true you were trying with the local council to get other accommodation on heath grounds?"

"Yes."

"On September 7 1952 you were working for British Road Services. Why did you leave, was it because of your poor health?"

"Yes."

"Did you tell Mr Burrow, a manager at British Road Services, that the reason you were leaving was because of your health?"

"Yes."

"He said you had got a job somewhere else, was that correct?"

"No, I said I might be going to Sheffield to look for work."

"Wherever you were going and whatever you said, could this be the reason for the killing of your wife?"

"No."

"Early on the morning of December 14 1952 you, without any motive, murdered your wife Ethel. You first claimed she was choking and convulsive. Then you said she took an overdose of phenobarbitone, which proved to be untrue at her post mortem. No traces of these drugs were found in her body. What did you do with your wife's body?"

"I left her in the bed and later put her under the floorboards in the front room."

"The letter to Ethel's sister Lily Bartle, September 10 1952. Did you alter this to September 15?"

"Yes."

"Why was this letter not posted on September 10?"

"Sometimes my wife would leave her letters lying around for days before they were completed."

"So this letter, like others, was left lying about?"

"Yes."

Judge Justice Finnemore then asked Christie how he had come by the letter.

"My wife used to leave unfinished letters in the writing drawer, and that's where I found it."

"Had she finished the letter?"

"Yes, but it had not been posted."

Examination continued: What reason did you have to alter the date to September 15?"

"Because I posted it on the 15th."

"By now, of course, your wife was dead."

"Yes."

"I suggest your action was to convince her relatives that she was still alive."

"No."

"Naturally they would think that everything was normal."

"Yes."

Judge Justice Finnemore: "You knew your wife was dead. Why were you doing this?"

"In my own mind I did not want to believe she was dead, I was trying to come to terms that she had gone and I had lost her."

Mr Curtis-Bennett continued his examination on the third day of the trial, Wednesday June 24.

"When did you first meet the prostitute Kathleen Maloney?"

"I think it was some time in January of this year. I was on my way home from getting some food for my cat and dog, then this woman came out from an alleyway and asked for some money and I said no. She followed me back to 10 Rillington Place, still demanding money, and started making a scene. Because of the neighbours I did not stop her when she forced her way inside."

"Then what happened?"

"She started to take off her clothes, to my disgust, because I found her utterly repulsive and she was drunk. She picked up a frying pan and tried to hit me with it."

"Did she manage to hit you?"

"No, I don't think so."

"You keep saying "think". Is this what you choose to remember now?"

"It is all rather vague at this moment, you see."

"Did you have sex with her?"

"Not then, as she still had the frying pan in her hand. I pushed her into the deckchair and I think I strangled her."

"What with?"

"I think it could have been a piece of cord or rope."

"Did you have sex with her then?"

"I don't remember."

Judge Justice Finnemore then asked Christie: "Will you tell the jury what reason you had to strangle this woman?"

"I don't know."

The examination continued. "Is this the case with all the women you killed?"

"Yes."

"What motive did you have against any of these women, or your wife?"

"None."

"Rita Nelson, another prostitute, where did you meet this woman."

"In a café."

"Was she by herself?"

"No, she was with another girl. I sat nearby and then Rita Nelson came over to me and asked if I had a cigarette. I said I did not smoke. She then went on to tell me they were looking for a place to live. I told her that I might be leaving 10 Rillington Place where I lived and there would be a vacant room."

"Did both these women go to 10 Rillington Place with you?"

"No, just Rita Nelson came in the evening. She asked if she could stay here until I left. I told her no. I think she then started to undress. I did not like this and I told her to clear off. She then became very violent, saying she would get in touch with some of the men she knew and they would sort me out."

"Did you have sex with her?"

"I cannot clearly remember all this."

"Then what did you do to her?"

"I strangled her and this is when I think I had intercourse with her."

"Had you at any time any reason or malice to hurt that woman?"

"No, I have never hurt anybody in my life."

"Kathleen Maloney, what did you do with her body?"

"Well, I have no idea."

"It is well known to this court that she was found in a cupboard in your kitchen, you know that now don't you?"

"I do not remember any of this, but I will accept what you say."

"Who else could have put her in that cupboard?"

"Well, I suppose it must have been me."

"How did Rita Nelson's body get in the cupboard?

"I don't remember there being an alcove."

"Who else could have put these women there?"

"I suppose it must have been me then."

"Do you agree that what happened to Rita Nelson took place on January 27 this year?"

"I have to accept that, but I cannot remember."

"You met Hectorina MacLennan and her boyfriend Mr Baker at the end of February this year, where did you meet them?"

"Outside a Notting Hill café."

"Did you know them?"

"No, they were complete strangers."

"What did they say to you?"

"Both of them appeared to be very upset. They were looking for a place to live as they had been told to leave their present accommodation by the weekend for not paying their rent. I said I might be able to put them up for a few days at 10 Rillington Place, until such time as they found somewhere else to live. After leaving them on that note I expected them to call sometime after the following weekend when they had to vacate their present lodgings. To my surprise they turned up the following day, Tuesday, at 2am, saying their landlady had turned them out that night."

"Was this the reason you all slept in the kitchen?"

"Yes."

"At that time, March 3 1953, the body of your wife Ethel was under the front room floorboards and also in the kitchen alcove were the bodies of the two prostitutes, all of whom you had murdered?"

"Yes."

"You all had your meals in this tiny kitchen for three days, where only a few feet away two bodies were probably beginning to decay in that alcove, and you allowed this couple to stay under these conditions for three nights?"

"Yes, I never gave it a thought."

"Did they stay on until the Friday?"

"Yes, but I did not like Baker, I told him he had to leave, I said Hectorina MacLennan could stay if she wanted to, but she went on to leave with Baker. However, she returned that night saying she had nowhere to go and could she stay here for a few days. I was very reluctant but I said yes. I then had second thoughts and told her she must leave. She refused to go and I pushed her towards the door. She resisted and there was a struggle. I caught hold of her round the neck and she went limp."

"Went limp?"

"Yes."

"Then what, did you strangle her?"

"I don't know, I must have done."

"Was she dead?

"I don't know."

"Do you remember having sex with her?"

"I might have done, but I can't recollect if I did."

"Do you remember putting her in the alcove?"

"No, I can't remember if I did this."

"Well who put her in there?"

"I just can't remember at this moment."

Judge Justice Finnemore: "At any time did Mr Baker come back to your house and speak to you?"

"I just can't remember, I just can't."

Examination continued: "You offered to sub-let your flat to a Mr and Mrs Reilly on about 15th or 16th March 1953?"

"Yes."

"You knew very well that the Reillys were going to occupy your flat and you were leaving behind four dead bodies, three concealed in your kitchen alcove and your wife under the floor boards in front living room?"

"Yes, but I never gave it a thought."

"You also took over £7 in advance for several weeks' rent. On the 20th March they moved in and you left."

"Yes."

"Did you go to Rowton House at Kings Cross?"

"I did not plan to go to a place like that, I really wanted to go back to 10 Rillington Place."

"But you could not go back to Rillington Place, you had sub-let it to the Reillys."

"I know that."

"So you had no choice but to go to Rowton House?"

"Yes."

"You produced your identity card and gave your address."

"Yes, that is correct."

"You were booked in to stay until March 27 and you stayed only until the 24th."

"I'm not sure how long I stayed there."

"Between March 24 and 31, what were you doing?"

"Well I don't remember, I must have been walking round and round in a kind of a daze."

"Then why did you leave Rowton House?"

"I don't know. I just walked out, I could not stand it there any longer."

"How did you get to Putney Embankment on March 31?

"I don't know."

"Can you remember being arrested on Putney Embankment?"

"Yes, I do remember a policeman coming up to me, asking for my name and if I had any identity on me."

"You gave him your name as being Waddington."

"I don't know what I said to him."

"In the van going to the police station did you not throw your wallet at the officer and said you can find my real name in there?"

"No, I did not throw anything, I do not behave in that manner."

"At Putney police station In the presence of Chief Inspector Griffin and Detective Inspector Kelly, you voluntarily made your first statement, is this true?"

"Yes, I was not put under any pressure at all."

"You gave an account of how your wife Ethel died, which seemed to be the same as you said here yesterday under oath."

"Yes, because that is the truth."

"Have you given a full account of these seven people and how they died?"

"I have done my best."

"Would you now say you are clear in your mind as to what exactly happened?"

"No, I don't think so."

"Have you killed anybody else besides those seven people?"

"I still can't remember, but if it was proven that I had then I will admit it."

Christie was then cross-examined by the Attorney General, who went over the full details of the evidence Christie had given to the court.

"With regard to the late Mrs Evans, firstly you denied you did not kill her and then, in other words, you said you did kill her. Is that correct?

"It can't be right."

"You have said two things that contradict each other."

"I don't know."

"Do you honestly think the jury is going to believe you?"

Christie did not reply to this.

Mr Curtis-Bennett then examined Dr Hobson, who said he had seen the defendant about twelve times. He told the court: "I think that when he was questioned over certain events he probably was unable to remember them, and then of course he may have chosen to lie. Christie, like so many murderers, has the ability to shut out all unpleasant things from his mind. He only remembers what suits him and what will help him."

Mr Curtis-Bennett then asked Dr Hobson if, when Christie told a story, he was forgetting.

"Yes, he does forget."

"And am I right in saying then, that in your view he never knew he was doing wrong when he committed these cruel acts?"

"Yes, that is so."

Two other eminent doctors, Dr Matherson and Dr Curran, gave evidence in which they said that they did not share Dr Hobson's opinion. That concluded the case for defence.

On the fourth day of the trial, Thursday June 25, Mr Curtis-Bennett made his closing speech for the defence. He went into great detail about Christie's case before asking the jury to find Christie guilty of the murder of his wife Ethel while insane.

Then the Attorney General gave his closing speech:

"It is not the law that every abnormal person with a mental disorder, as was suggested in Christie's case, should expect a verdict of guilty but insane. Christie knew what he was doing when killing his wife and five prostitutes. Therefore, the defence has been unable to prove their case that Christie was insane at the time he murdered his wife."

Mr Justice Finnemore then asked the jury to retire and consider their verdict. The jury took one hour and 20 minutes to find Christie guilty.

The judge then pronounced the sentence of death. Christie was to be hanged on July 15 1953.

Chapter Eight

AFTERMATH

Following the trial there was a general outcry by some Members of Parliament and the general public over the fact that Timothy Evans had been hanged when it now appeared he was very likely innocent. An enquiry was called, and it opened on Monday July 6 1953, chaired by John Scott Henderson. There was some urgency, because Christie was due to be hanged in nine days' time.

Mr Gillis was the solicitor acting on behalf of Evans' mother, Mrs Probert, who at the enquiry asked to see the transcript of the statements taken from the witnesses at Evans' trial and to cross-examine the witnesses. These two requests were refused.

Mr Scott Henderson interviewed the Notting Hill police with regard to the confessions Evans had made. He accepted as true Evans' confession in one of his statements that he had killed his wife and child. He was of the opinion that it had shown first-hand knowledge of the crime.

He interviewed Christie in prison and rejected his confession that he had murdered Mrs Evans. He was convinced that Christie was still trying to prove he was insane, and that his story of gassing Mrs Evans was totally untrue, as was proven at her post-mortem. Christie's statements were unreliable and full of lies.

Mr Scott Henderson recalled that Evans had claimed he had put the bodies of Beryl and her baby in the wash-house on Tuesday November 8 1949 - this was in the first statement he had made at Notting Hill Police Station. He went on to interview one of the workmen who was repairing the wash-house roof at that time, and from what he was told he was satisfied that no bodies had been in the wash-house on that date. It was clear that the bodies had been placed in the wash-house after November 8.

No bodies could therefore have been put in the wash-house on November 8 as Evans claimed. Mr Jones confirmed to Mr Scott Henderson that they were still working on the wash-house roof that day and they were constantly in and out of the building. He said no bodies could have possibly been in there as the wash-house was so small. If they had been there on that date, especially baby Geraldine behind the door, they would have been discovered. It is evident that on this Evans was again lying.

Mr Scott Henderson's conclusion was that the case against Timothy John Evans had been overwhelming, and he was quite satisfied that there had been no miscarriage of justice. Evans had indeed been responsible for the deaths of his wife and daughter.

His report however came under severe criticism from members of the House of Commons, some saying it was a whitewash and dishonest and demanding a further inquiry. Parliament refused, and as far they were concerned it was the end of the matter.

Many people in England were not happy about this. To admit that an innocent man had been hanged would have meant the end of the death penalty, and at that time the Government no doubt wanted it to remain.

But then two years later, Ruth Ellis was hanged for the murder of her lover, David Blakely; she had shot him outside a public house called the Magdala in Hampstead on Easter Sunday 10th April 1955. There were calls again for the death penalty to be abolished. The last hanging took place in England in 1964. After that, capital punishment was suspended. On December 16 1969 the Home Secretary, James Callaghan, proposed a motion to make the Act permanent, and the death penalty was finally abolished in England in 1969.

Following the revelations at the Christie trial, Mrs Probert made a request to her MP and the very young Queen Elizabeth II for permission to have her son's remains moved to holy ground at St Patrick's Cemetery at Leytonstone, Essex. Her request was granted.

In 1965-66 a further enquiry took place into the Evans case. It produced the following statement from Mr Justice Brabin: "I have come to the conclusion that it is more probable than not that Evans killed Beryl Evans. I have come to the conclusion that it is more probable than not that Evans did not kill Geraldine."

In 2003, granting Evans' sisters compensation for the 'wrongful execution' of Evans, Lord Brennan QC, the independent assessor for the Home Office, stated: "the conviction and execution of Timothy Evans for the murder of his child was wrongful and a miscarriage of justice… there is no evidence to implicate Timothy Evans in the murder of his wife. She was most probably murdered by Christie." Lord Brennan believed that the Brabin Report's conclusion that Evans probably murdered his wife should be rejected, given Christie's confessions and conviction.

On November 16 2004 an appeal was made by Evans' sisters to the High Court to overturn a decision not to refer Timothy Evans' case to the court of appeal to have his conviction formally quashed. On November 19 2004 the judges said the cost and resources involved in quashing the conviction could not be justified, and it still remains today.

John Reginald Halliday Christie was hanged on July 15 1953. As he was prepared for execution he complained that his nose itched. The hangman, Albert Pierrepoint, who had also been Evans' executioner, told Christie: "Don't worry, it won't bother you for long".

Christie and Evans had both behaved in the same manner after killing their wives. Both lied as to their whereabouts, sold their wedding rings and all their personal possessions and, on the face of it, showed no remorse. However, there was some difference between these two men. Christie was a seasoned killer. Murder was easy for him, and he had an unhealthy obsession with dead bodies. His hatred of women was immense, probably due to the domination of his five sisters. His father did not help by his cruel treatment of the young Christie.

What turned this apparently quiet man into a monster? The causes go back to a series of events during his life. Christie's failure to perform sexually played on his mind, and the taunting he got from women led to his dealing with prostitutes. It was not until eighteen years after he married Ethel and moved to 10 Rillington Place that his murderous, perverted urges began to surface.

When the Evans family came into his life he set out on the road to the gallows. What he did during those years was diabolical.

We shall never know for sure whether or not Christie killed Beryl and Geraldine Evans. As I have said before, I do not believe he did. More than likely he had lecherous thoughts about Beryl; she was a lovely young girl. But that is as far as he could go. Whatever one may think about Evans, his presence stopped Christie from going one step beyond.

When it came to hiding his victims, Christie more or less shot himself in the foot. The way the bodies were dealt with was clumsy to say the least. The first two were buried in the garden, in shallow graves. A thigh bone was found propping up the fence, Christie's dog dug up one of the skulls and Christie took it away and casually threw it on to a London bomb site, where it was found later by children playing there.

As for the three victims dumped in the kitchen alcove - how long could Christie have hoped to leave them there? The smell would soon have become unbearable. Yet he moved out of 10 Rillington Place and left behind all the evidence of his crimes. He must have realised it would only be a matter of time before the bodies were found, as indeed it was. One must wonder if Christie's mind was in a state of confusion. However, if he had escaped the law I feel sure he would have gone on to murder yet more women.

There is a widespread consensus that the police bungled their investigations in the Evans case, failing to search the premises systematically and overlooking the most obvious evidence. A proper search would surely have uncovered the bodies of Ruth Fuerst and Muriel Eady, and whatever the outcome of the Evans trial, Christie would never have been left free to murder his wife and the three other women.

Christie was like a cornered rat, and a very dangerous one. He certainly earned himself a place in the history books, which is just what he would have wanted. We can be sure no sad laments will be sung for John Reginald Halliday Christie.

Timothy John Evans appears to me to have been a lost soul, pathetic and immature. He never knew his father, who had walked out on the family before he was born. There is no doubt in my mind that Evans killed his wife and daughter. He became a killer through circumstances beyond his control. His violent temper and lies were always going to be his downfall.

I believe Evans got his own way whenever it suited him, and if he did not he resorted to losing his temper. His family accepted that his lies were part of his nature and nothing could be done about it. To punish him was certainly not the answer. They had to live with his temper, or perhaps they did not care.

When Evans married in 1947, times were hard. The country was staggering to its feet after six long years of war and people lived from one Friday payday to the next. What little you possessed, you appreciated. Evans and his wife started married life in a back bedroom in his mother's house. He had no problems there, as we know, but after the move to 10 Rillington Place the ups and downs of married life became a reality and every penny he was to earn was accounted for.

Some of Evans' employers said he was a hard worker. He certainly had a long day, from 6.30 am to 7 pm. Other employers found him lazy and said he was always asking for an advance on his wages. He was always borrowing money which he never paid back.

The claim that Evans was illiterate was not entirely true. Until he was 24 he does not appear to have had any problems. He lived with his mother, and it is more then likely she never took much of his wages. He was able to pursue the lifestyle that suited him. He went often to join his friends for drinking sessions at The Kensington Park Hotel, and he liked going to the dog track and the cinema. Therefore his home life should have been free from stress. If at any time he needed more money his mother was always there to help out.

It was never known how well he got on with his stepfather; one can only make a guess. Mrs Probert fought hard to save her son's life. She honestly believed him when he said it was Christie who had murdered Beryl and the baby. She went so far as to plead with Christie to own up that he had killed them both, but it was no use.

Whether her son was guilty or not, it must have been a dreadful ordeal for her. Her one wish was to see his conviction squashed, which never happened. The only source of comfort to her was that after the abolition of the death penalty in 1965 she was given permission to move her son's body to holy ground. The following year he won his posthumous pardon, though his conviction has never been overturned.

The years following Evans' hanging must have been very traumatic for her and the family – it was a tragic end to a young man's life and he left behind dreadful memories. Some compassion could be felt for the late Timothy John Evans; he was a victim of his own nature and background.

Beryl Thorley was just eighteen years old when she married Evans – too young, in the view of many people. True, today many young girls go into relationships and have babies at a much younger age, but in those days things were much harder. The war had not long ended and there was not the state support that is available today. Evans' mother had to help them out by paying their wedding expenses. The only money they had was Evans' wages at the end of each week. Beryl became pregnant very quickly, so she was thrown in at the deep end.

When they went to live at 10 Rillington Place the conditions there were appalling. How this young girl managed during her first pregnancy is a mystery. Then when her baby daughter Geraldine was barely ten months old she found herself again pregnant, and by all accounts she was devastated. She did her best to try to end this unwanted pregnancy, but to no avail.

The arrival of baby Geraldine was just about all they were able to cope with, though she was loved by all. One cannot help wondering why then did Evans not use a form of birth control to prevent another baby arriving?

Condoms were available at all chemists. Again we hear of his lack of consideration towards Beryl and his heartless comment when told of this second baby: "You had one, another won't make any difference".

I have to draw attention again to the mystery that surrounds Beryl's mother, Elizabeth Simmonds. It was always said that during Beryl's marriage her mother had died, with no mention of when or how. Then in 1949 at the home of Beryl's grandmother, Mrs Barnett, a Miss Simmonds (no mention of a Christian name) appeared during a police interview, saying she was Mrs Barnett's daughter.

Many unkind things were said about Beryl after her death. Mrs Probert claimed she saw her hanging out the washing in the garden at 10 Rillington Place when Christie suddenly appeared and put his arm around her. It was suggested that Beryl was having an affair with Christie. Yet under the tenancy agreement Beryl had no access to the garden and furthermore there was no such washing line - the so-called 'garden' was nothing but a mass of rubbish. Under Christie's tenancy agreement he had sole use of the garden, and he made sure this was adhered to. He guarded the secrets he had buried in the garden with his life.

Beryl had a very short life, and her final years were fraught with poverty and problems. I am saddened by the fact that Beryl and her baby daughter Geraldine were not laid to rest in a grave of their own at Gunnersbury Cemetery in London. Instead they were buried in a common grave. The first name on the headstone was a George Henry Potter, who happened to have died about the same time – he had no connection with Beryl and her baby daughter. But at least their names were added to the headstone.

Baby Geraldine's murder at fourteen months of age was tragic. We also have to remember that the little boy Beryl was carrying died too on that fatal night of Tuesday November 8 1949. May these young victims forever rest in peace.

A question I must ask. If before Evans' trial the police had searched the garden properly and Christie's earlier murders had been discovered, would

Evans have been convicted and hanged? In my view he might well not have been. He said in some of his statements that he had helped Christie to carry his wife's body down the stairs into Mr Kitchener's flat. If we are to believe this and knowing the lies that Evans was capable of telling, he knew his wife was dead, and this would have made him an accessory before and after the fact. At the least he would have faced a long prison sentence, and perhaps considered for parole in later years.

The evidence in the case was highly conflicting, to the extent that we shall never know for sure exactly what happed in that ghastly house. Four people between them knew the truth; John Christie, his wife Ethel, Beryl Evans and Timothy John Evans, and they all took their secrets with them to the grave.

Perhaps that is where they belong. If we knew the full truth I suspect we would probably be even more shocked, if that were possible.

Let us remember all those victims, especially baby Geraldine Evans. None of them deserved to die in such a violent way. It has been said many times that some houses can be evil, but I have to say I don't believe this. It is people who make a house evil, and that is what Christie and Evans did to 10 Rillington Place.

The address became so notorious that within a few months of the trial, in response to a petition from the remaining residents, it was renamed Ruston Close. The change of name did not stop a stream of tourists and souvenir hunters visiting the place to see for themselves the house which had seen so much death.

Under any name, Rillington Place has long gone; the street was demolished in the early 1970s. Today modern houses stand there, and it is now called St Andrew's Square. The tranquil setting is graced by trees and shrubs. But does this help to blot out what once stood there? The past will always remain in our memories.